The Secret 52 Star Codes of Creation

The Stellar Guidebook

52 Star Codes Book Series

Book 1

Karyn Chabot Martino

Copyright

❀ Created with Vellum

Contents

Gratitude   vii

Author's Note   1
Preface   3
Introduction   9
How To Use This Book   17
Are You a Cusper?   23
Genesis of the Suits: The Ankh   26
Evolution of the Suits   35
Star Code Terminology   37
All the Layers   78
When a Card Appears   84
Soul Genealogy   90
The Reign of the 8 of Diamonds   98
Golden Rule   102
Stargate Exploration   104
Stargate Birthdays   108
Stargate Case Study   116
The Mother Wound   125
Genders and the Suits   134
The Trine of Deception   138
Favorable and Unfavorable Planetary Cycles   140
Hallowed Be Thy Name: Letter Values   145
Star Codes Composites   150
Composite Instructions   153
The Black Hole: 9/6 Portal   155
The Blue Hole: 2/6 Portal   162
The Ace-Ten Exchange   167
The Two Presence Healers of The Deck   170
Ho'oponopono Forgiveness Novena   175
Reasons to Forgive Your Parents   177
The Stellar Forgiveness Novena   178

52 Star Code Worksheet   183
Birthday Card Directory   192

About the Author   207

Dedication

To heal the Mother Wound within you, begin by
mourning the loss of the fantasy of the mother
you wish you had.

I dedicate this book to my daughter,
mother, and beloved grandmothers and
all those affected by the Mother Wound in
our family lineage and soul genealogy.
We are not alone in this healing,
understanding, and forgiveness journey.
May my unborn grandchildren be free
from this affliction and have the most
rewarding and loving relationship with
their mother and all mother-like figures. May the wisdom on
these pages heal all the Readers who also have the Mother
Wound. I thank the Divine Mother for blessing and healing each
person who reads this book. I also devote this book to all
sensitive and sentient beings journeying a challenging life path
and seeking navigation tools that will help them elevate, ignite
their inner knowing, remember, and become the best version of
themselves while finding happiness on their road toward self
discovery and love.

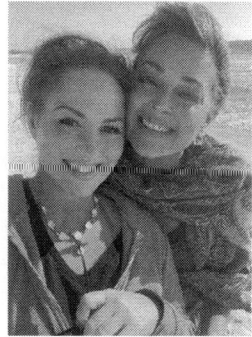

Gratitude

Living in a state of gratitude is the gateway to grace. - Arianna Huffington

Thank you to all the people who helped me write this book. I could not have done this without you. I am infinitely grateful to my beloved husband, Daniel Martino, for tolerating all my disappearances into my writing cave and cheering me on. Thank you to my gifted friend and Shaman teacher, Annette Burke, for channeling some of the new cognitions in this book. Thank you to Puma, my cat, for creating a 9/6 portal, inviting mystical messages to come through as he sat by my side the entire time I wrote this book. Thank you to my friends, clients, and family who agreed to be part of this book with their photos, bio, and personal stories about their cards. Thank you to my student, Iona Ross, for helping develop a massive chart with all the new Star Code terminology. Thank you to Jennifer Bramley and Lauren Bentley for editing and being the wind beneath my wings.

Thank you to the Stone People, who gifted me a stone during a walking meditation on one of the Rhode Island beaches in 2024. The perfect diamond shape carved into it, a testament to their role as the record keepers of the earth, has left a lasting impression on this book.

Thank you to the Sacred Gatekeepers of this 52 Star Code System. Your wisdom, shared as my fingers typed and during my meditations, has revolutionized this system. Your ancient truths revealed through my humble request, have added depth and richness to this book.

Thank you to all my teachers, including Robert Lee Camp, David Suchy, Thomas Morrell, David Hawthorne, Penelope Farrow, Renay Oshop, Dr. Vasant Lad, and many other Ayurvedic Astrology teachers and colleagues. Thank you to Meghan Greer for gifting me with Robert Lee Camp's card software in 2006. Thank you to my brilliant Eight of Club's soul sister Katya for her contagious passion for this System in 2004.

> Stones are alive, but they are in a sweet coma. - Dr. Vasant Lad

Author's Note

Thank you for reading my book. I hope it provides profound insights into who you are and the relationships that have made you who you are today.

Dear Friends,

This is a five-book series. The primary book, The Stellar Guidebook, is designed to explain the details in the other four books, each dedicated to the Heart, Clubs, Diamonds, and Spades suits. The Stellar Guidebook is an integral part of the series; it may not be easy to understand the other books without it.

To deepen your knowledge of the 52 Star Code System, enroll in my Star Code School online and become a certified Star Coder. I invite you to join my newsletter using the QR code above and enter a raffle to win a free 30-minute Star Code reading with me. As a subscriber, you'll gain access to exclusive discounts for 1:1 sessions with me, tuition deductions, and scholarships. By joining, you become part of a community that values personal growth. I would be grateful if you also left me an Amazon Book Review on *The Stellar Guidebook* with my 5-book series. All Love, Karyn

Preface

No man can reveal to you aught but that which already lies half-asleep in the dawning of your knowledge. - Kahlil Gibran

Cards? Really? I grew up in an Ivy League Catholic home where "card" was a four-letter word. I rejected the idea of learning how to read the deck of playing cards in 2004 because I associated them with gambling, gypsies, and other shenanigans. I was on a devoted dharmic path, raising my vibration, healing my clients, and teaching Ayurvedic medicine and massage. Cards were not part of that, so I thought. They were a distraction and a waste of precious time. What happened to me? How did I change my childhood programming? It wasn't easy.

I was first introduced to the cards by a dear friend, Katya, whom I met in Costa Rica at Puravida Resorts while training the staff there in Ayurvedic bodywork. Katya was in my training and considered one of the resort's most revered healers. She is a certified Bodytalk Systems practitioner on the yogic path of dharma, purity, and service. We got along great and respected each other's work. I invited her to stay with me in Newport, RI, for three months in 2005 and set her up with all my beloved and loyal massage and Ayurveda clients. They loved her!

In addition to the miraculous Bodytalk healings Katya

performed with my trusted clients while she was visiting, each client confided that the last ten minutes of Katya's Bodytalk sessions were their favorite. Why? Because she read everyone's cards and made stellar predictions that all came true! She was brilliant, intuitive, and relentlessly encouraging me to read Robert Lee Camp's Love Cards and Cards of Destiny books.

I asked myself, "How could all my clients report the same story about Katya's cards?" Not one of them said a negative thing. They begged me to do their cards after Katya returned to Costa Rica. I didn't know how, but I could no longer dismiss it. Katya came for another visit, and we drenched ourselves in Camp's books and cards. It was so much fun to do together and mind-blowingly insightful. It changed my world by inspiring me to forgive those who hurt me, especially family members, and giving me reasons to forgive myself. Studying the cards helped me understand some of the tragedies in my life more clearly. My twenty years of massage and Ayurveda Health practice slowly evolved into my new passion: 52-Star Code System and Vedic Medical Astrology. Thanks to my friend and soul sister, Katya, a genius Eight of Clubs.

Nineteen years later, I wrote this book to bring this sacred language of the stars to the world and revolutionize the system. I want to help people understand themselves, their lives, and others around them more clearly. It's a remarkable navigational tool for life, so why wouldn't I want to share that? I don't claim to know all the answers, but I discovered some profound clues to life's mysteries inside the 52-Star Code System. In the pages of this book, I endeavor to explain how fate and destiny dance together in time, using the power of resonate frequency embedded within each card. When we understand everything is frequency, the universe becomes a symphony.

The first and most profound gift this 52-Star Code System gave me was a better "understanding" of my family, myself, and my relationships. We can forgive and stop shaming and blaming ourselves and others through understanding. This system's second most profound gift was to sharpen my intuition through validation, thus opening my third eye more widely as I continue to learn to trust the whispers in my heart. The whispers in my heart usually align with the harmonics within my card spreads. When that happens to anyone using any divination system, we recognize it as truth. Truth can be a rare commodity in our world, with all the lies poisoning the news and social media. The good news is that the 52-Star Code System doesn't lie.

This wisdom in this book portrays how we are infinitely boundless, unique as a snowflake, and not limited to one or two cards or codes. Many more hidden formulas have yet to be re-discovered inside this 52-Star Code System. This book is just the tip of the iceberg. I hope this book inspires my readers, clients, and students to continue to chip away at the iceberg. I hope they continue decoding this system's secrets over time, with or without me, because the world could be better with this sacred knowledge. We can continue to brainstorm, cognize, download, and intuit the missing pieces and demystify the magic imbued within the pages of this book and beyond.

Each Star Code acts like a portal, favorable or unfavorable. Portals are harmonic doorways into life's mysteries. My mission is to find the keys to using this system so that we can manifest our dreams by discovering how to open each portal utilizing the power of intention. We may not only use this system to predict our potential futures— yes, that's plural because we all have many futures depending on our consciousness—but also to transform our futures and open new, more beautiful, and rewarding futures. The idea of "intention" and "vibrational card activation using thought" is similar to what people do with the power of prayer, meditation, and the laws of attraction. Thoughts are prayers.

It is rare to achieve any of the goals mentioned above using written statements or arguments since, to the suspended judgment of my readers, it always seems plausible to say that the author was dishonest or delusional and, therefore, the evidence was tainted. I have intentionally omitted all persuasive arguments and irrefutable evidence. Instead, I challenge the open-hearted reader to practice the codes of consciousness revealed in this book. Personal revelations and success will prove far more conclusive than all the literary work on this subject. This book would be many times its size if it could transfer sentiment and faith to my readers by employing persuasive statements or Ivy League references.

As you absorb the unfolding magic of this book, notice the luminous flashes of recognition and clarity that light up your mind, igniting memories and imprints in the seat of your soul from time immemorial. Somewhere inside, you may say, "Aha, I knew that!" Kahlil Gibran eloquently said, "No man can reveal to you aught but that which already lies half-asleep in the dawning of your knowledge." Suddenly, grace appears with your newfound awareness as the words on each page resonate with you, marking the genesis of a new chapter in your world where you make more informed, liberated, and empowered decisions while beginning to forgive yourself and others.

If we wrote our script for each lifetime, why would it not share similarities within the archetypal meanings of the Jacks, Queens, and Kings in a deck of cards? "All the world's a stage, and all the men and women merely players. They have their exits and entrances, and one man in his time plays many parts." – Shakespeare. Each secret Star Code is disguised as a card, hiding in plain sight, as a numerical and cosmic value, all in the same breath.

Since we live in a world of duality, where we have two eyes, two arms, two legs, and so on, this concept of duality is instilled within each Star Code. Each code has its own story and a dark and a light expression, sometimes expressing both all at once, and sometimes how it will play out depends on how the planetary cycles influence the cards and how your state of consciousness perceives the energy. According to Vedic scripture, even the cosmos itself is rooted in the myth of the ancient planetary war between the Asuras and the Devas, which gives rise to the celestial divide in the sky and defines intrinsically favorable and unfavorable planets. Read more about this in the chapter titled "Favorable and Unfavorable."

This notion supports the adage, "As above, so below."- The Kybalion. Our bodies are microcosms of the macrocosm, embodying the entire galaxy within us, down to the cellular and quantum levels. The yin and yang symbol explains the paradox of how the black fish chases the white fish in a perpetual circle, signifying the union of lightness and darkness on the karmic wheel of life. There would be no white fish without the blackfish and vice versa. Both are necessary to survive on this planet.

Our brains want to immediately classify things, including cards, as good or bad so they can quickly dismiss them and move on. In my readings, after explaining my client's natal card, about 80 percent of my clients' first question is, "Is that good or bad?" My reply is always the same, "There is no dedicated or defined good or bad card or Star Code in this system, just as there are no good or bad snowflakes. They are just beautifully different. Shakespeare knew this well when he said, "The web of our life is of a mingled yarn, good and ill together."

This 52-Star Code System can quickly become an addiction if you let it. However, please do not give your power to it or obsess over it. These cards have no power over you, as you are an infinite and powerful being capable of happiness without these cards. However, I have found that by learning to read and interpret the language of these 52 Star Codes, my intuition has heightened, my confidence enhanced, and my ability to under-stand, love, and forgive myself and others has exponentially risen. Upon studying this system in 2003, I realized I spent half my life being blind-sided, shocked, disappointed, and dismayed by many people, relationships, events, and emotions. Why should we walk around in the dark? I am immensely grateful for this little, unbound guidebook to living a conscious, happy life disguised inside a deck of cards.

The cosmos reflects conditioned consciousness objectified. Consciousness is the cause, and vocabulary is the fabric of life. So, it is to consciousness that we must seek our answers to discover the secret of creation. Yes, every Star Code has a river of consciousness because we are the Stardust of the Universe.

> Above the cloud with its shadow is a star with its light. Above all things, reverence thyself. - Pythagoras

Introduction

"All that is required to realize the self is to 'Be Still.'- Ramana Maharshi

The deck of 52 playing cards is a divine compilation of ancient hidden codes handed to humans from highly evolved extra-terrestrials called the Anunnaki. I channeled this information one day while lying on my mother's soft carpeted floor under her cathedral ceiling after a sumptuous Thanksgiving dinner. In my third eye, I "heard" this in an alpha state and wondered who the Anunnaki were. I had heard about this race at some point years ago but never thought twice about it. My curiosity inspired me to research this finding at a deeper level after I received that download. I discovered a common theme from numerous cred-ible sources claiming they taught early humans about sacred geometry and spiritual mathematics. That resonated with my logical mind, and I trust my Guides.

These codes are the keys to understanding life on planet Earth. There are 52 weeks in a year, 52 cards in the deck, four seasons, and four suits. There are 12 months, 12 court cards, 13 cards in each suit, 13 weeks in each season, and 13 lunar cycles each year. When we add all the Star Codes of each card, they total 364. The Joker brings the total to 365, the number of days in the year.

In this book, I will interchange the terms Code and Card, as they mean the same. Let's break down the word Card C=29, a=1, r=18, d=4. 29+1+18+4=52. King of Spades is the last card in the deck of 52 Cards, whose Star Code is 52. Next, break down the word Code: C=29, o=15, d=4, e=5. 29+15+4+5=53. When subtracting 52 from 53, we get #1, whose Star Code is Ace of Hearts. Ace of Hearts is the very first card in the deck. January 1 is the only birthday of the King of Spades. December 30 is the only birthday of the Ace of Hearts. December 31 reflects the Joker but contains the Ace of Hearts and King of Spades, separating the day in half. December 31 is akin to the sunrise and sunset between the day and night. It is the Savasana at the end of a yoga class. It represents the sacred silence between the inhale and the exhale.

To understand these Star Codes as a mystical calendar, we must recognize the following serendipitous peculiarities: There are 52 cards representing the 52 weeks in the year. Two colors, red and black, represent the duality on Earth, such as day versus night or masculine versus feminine. There are four suits representing the four seasons. There are thirteen weeks per season and thirteen lunations each year. There are twelve court cards representing the twelve calendar months. If we add the Star Code Values of each card, it totals 364. See the Star Code Letter Value Chart at the back of this book. Even if we had 13 months in a year and 13 cosmic constellations, the 52-Star Code System still applies.

A deck of cards reveals the perfect order of life, starting at the Ace of Hearts (birth) and ending at the King of Spades (death). The cards are then strategically placed, honoring the four directions to create the Earth Template. This process is called "Quadrating." After this process, the cards are laid out in seven planetary rows and columns, with the last three cards placed in the center across the top, denoting the crown line. The cards are then returned to their original order and laid out repeatedly to form the subsequent templates for each year in the life of a human. These are the sacred 90 templates representing each year of our lives that are the foundation of the 52-Star Code System.

This system has helped release the blame and shame from the game of life by revealing insights about interpersonal relationships with family and loved ones. Most importantly, it unveiled my relationship with myself and what makes me who I am relative to the rest of the world. The key word is 'relative'. You see, life is all about relationships. Dr. Vasant Lad, BAM, one of my most profound teachers of wisdom and Ayurvedic medicine, understood this principle beautifully. In 1997, I attended The Ayurvedic Institute, where he was my first Ayurvedic instructor and doctor. When I had a medical consultation with him, his first question was, "How is your relationship?" I assumed he meant with a romantic partner, but he also meant the relationship with myself.

I was surprised he didn't ask about my physical health first because I was from a very traditional Western allopathic background that did not incorporate the body, mind, and spirit dynamic. Later, I discovered that "How is your relationship?" is the first question Dr. Lad asks every client. Brilliant. He also told his 1998 class, "The root cause of all disease is to be in a confused relationship." Even more brilliant. The 52-Star Code System helps illuminate truth, remove confusion, sharpen intuition, and create healthier, more loving relationships.

We can use these codes for divination and seeing into the past and future. More importantly, this system provides tools for understanding our family dynamics, loved ones, neighbors, colleagues, and all other significant relationships. We can also use them to track missing persons, solve murder mysteries, avoid unfavorable situations and people, choose auspicious timing for important events, and understand when and how to heal ourselves best.

Since the principles of relationship interface with the concept of duality, it is essential to open and examine at least two or more card charts for your client or yourself simultane- ously. Why? Because the language of the 52-Star Code System can only be interpreted and understood at the emotional level and maturity of the querent. Suppose, in the worst-case scenario, you are reading for a sociopath. They are often delu- sional and have no idea how to emote. For example, what they perceive as joyful may differ from what you perceive as joyful, so we can't assume. If you read only your client's chart for insights, your interpretations may be skewed because you don't know how to feel or think like a sociopath. Using a second chart rela- tive to the querent will balance your reading. This example is of the worst-case scenario. It's not up to us to determine whether a client is a sociopath or not, but this practice puts us in a safe zone, just in case, and gives us an edge.

I always open my clients' charts first, then ask them for someone who loves them so I can create a chart of that person, too. That second chart is not FOR the other person. It is for me to track my client in the other's chart. When we read the chart of someone who cares about them, we will have an expanded awareness of the truth and a reality check. Sometimes, I will pull up the charts of an entire family for one client to get the most comprehensive understanding. Opening two or more charts also provides confluence. One of my most outstanding Vedic astrology teachers, Hart de Fouw, gave me a reading in 1998 at The Ayurvedic Institute in NM and opened at least five of my family member's charts just for my reading. I still have notes from that reading, and everything he predicted was 100 percent accurate. I tell my clients and students that most oracles, astrology, and psychic readings will only be about 85 percent correct. I give the 52-Star Code System about 95 percent accuracy based on my years of experience. Still, the accuracy will depend upon the reader's state of consciousness, intuitive gifts, and ability to interpret the language of the stars.

I often read others directly through the charts of the ones that love them most. Some of my best predictions have been from reading for people through their beloved pets' eyes. Animals are pure-hearted and usually not delusional. They have feelings, too, and their owners can be seen and mathematically tracked precisely in their pets' charts if you have their birthday.

Each star code has a mathematically measurable harmonic. These ancient archetypal codes give rise to life's once-forbidden symbolic language of the stars and nature. They were once banned because they were a threat to the nefarious leaders, royalty, and power-driven authorities who wanted to use lies to manipulate and instill fear to control the masses. Anyone caught using the language of the 52-Star Code System faced persecution because the system was much too powerful, and the beguiling leaders could not compete. These were and still are Star Codes of profound truth and accuracy, resembling a mystical calendar of time. Thankfully, the Gatekeepers of these sacred Star Codes kept the system alive by hiding them in plain sight under the clever guise of unassuming card games like poker, bridge, and go-fish.

Unfortunately, the word "card" has inherited a bad rap for many reasons listed above, but also because cards have been misused for dark purposes, associated with gypsies, gambling, and misdirected fortune tellers with ego-driven agendas. People have called weirdos a "card" as an insult or referred to someone's way of life as a "House of Cards." I aim to revolutionize that outdated, fear-based paradigm and help my readers understand that the insights the 52-Star Code System may reveal can improve our lives dramatically. This insight may help us make informed daily choices and help us love and forgive ourselves and one another while witnessing the mysterious dualistic play of life on Earth.

The year we are in as I publish this book, the Earth is at the cusp of the Kali Yuga, a Sanskrit term for "dark ages." The planet is about to transition into the Sat Yuga, another Sanskrit term for "age of truth," and the dawn of the seventh golden age of enlightenment. Once we fully enter the Sat Yuga, we will work with a NEW Earth Template, which I will disclose in my 52 Star Code Student Guide. In 1752, the Gregorian Calendar replaced the Julian Calendar, changing the formula for calculating leap years. When this calendar change occurred, the genesis of the new year was switched from March 25 to January 1. Finally, 11 days were dropped from September 1752, distorting the truth about time and the coherence in our calendars. Yet, despite all these changes, the 52-Star Code System still applies. I hope we drop the twisted Gregorian calendar and adopt a new one in the Sat Yuga to help humans connect more deeply with nature, love, peace, sunshine, health, and all sacred things outside this time-space continuum.

Astrology, numerology, divination, and mysticism are ancient but still vital disciplines practiced and valued by cultures world-wide. The observation and study of the heavens reveal a mean-ingful and influential correlation between the position and motion of the planets, stars, and other celestial phenomena and our lives. Astrology rests upon the central spiritual premise of reincarnation. The belief is that the soul picks the precise time, place, and family to be born into to create the opportunity to fulfill its highest potential and resolve unfinished business from past lives.

A modern, in-depth examination of a person from an astrological perspective is a much more individualized, complex, layered, and sophisticated analysis than broad-stroke-sign-based Astrology, typically found in newspapers or magazines. A more individualized approach, using the 52-Star Code System, can provide us with profound psychological and spiritual insight. A study of the position of the heavenly bodies at the moment of our birth, the natal horoscope, provides us with a symbolic map of our psyche and a blueprint for our soul's evolution. Understanding this map can provide:

- Insight into ourselves and others
- Our strengths
- Our vulnerabilities
- Essential messages and guidance about our life purpose, traits, and direction

This map represents our potential and not who we are in a static or fixed way. It is not fated; instead, it illuminates our choices in the most boundless way. The study of the way the heavens can influence our lives can empower us by increasing our conscious awareness of the energies of the moment. It puts us in a better position to harness these energies and flow with them rather than waste opportunities or struggle against them. This awareness enhances personal freedom and choice and compassion for the self and others. It enables us to become conscious of our true potential and how we needlessly limit ourselves.

This card system is subjective, not objective, so opening two card charts for your client is essential, as I mentioned at the beginning of this introduction. One chart should be of someone who knows them deeply and cares for or loves them. The other chart should be the querent's birth chart. This practice aligns with a powerful principle called 'confluence.' The Oxford Dictionary defines this principle as: "A flowing together; the junction and union of two or more streams or moving fluids." If life interfaces with the notion of relationship, then life is also rooted in confluence. May we all flow harmoniously, be mirrors for one another, and help walk each other home.

> *What if our religion was each other? If our practice was our life. If prayer, our words. What if the temple was the Earth? If forests were our church. If holy water--the rivers, lakes, and ocean. What if meditation was our relationship? If the teacher was life. If wisdom was self knowledge. If love was the center of our being. ~ Ganga White*

How To Use This Book

In the sunlight of awareness, all things become
sacred. -Thich Nhat Hahn

Most people use astrology, cards, and divination systems to
predict the future, understand the past, and understand themselves. However, this divination system offers all of the above
plus the opportunity to maneuver fate and destiny using free
will, intentionality, and consciousness. I discovered this while
writing this book. How? While I wrote each chapter on each
unique card, I found myself fully entrenched in that particular
card, thinking of all the people and clients I knew who had that
card and all the meanings of each card. As I did this over the
last two years of writing this book, I can say with 100 percent
conviction that someone who embodied that particular card
would text, email, call, or show up at my door, sometimes immediately or within a few hours. Yes, it happens that fast!

During the first year of observing this magical discovery, I
wondered if the powers of fate knew I would be working on that
card on that day, at that moment, or if I was opening portals to
that vibration of that card by immersing myself in the meaning
of its signification and writing about it. Once the portal to that

card opened using the power of thought, many people associated with it would appear. It was the classic chicken before the egg plight for the first year of writing this book. It seems all great discoveries happen by accident because that's exactly how this unfolded while writing this book.

This part of the 52-Star-Code System is all new to me. It's a massive breakthrough. What does this mean? We may manifest what we want by concentrating on the cards that most describe our desires. For example, suppose you are missing or worried about someone and wish they would contact you. First, you'd have to find out their birthday. Once you find that, research all their layers, starting with the External birth card. Then, immerse yourself in their birth card's meanings, fully digesting it so that the card's meanings and secret codes become so clear to you that it feels tangible. Then, expect contact from that person within 24 hours or less! If that doesn't work, choose one of their other layers, like their Internal card. It also helps if you think of or associate that person with the card as you immerse yourself in the card's significance. I would ask that you practice this with only pure and good intentions; otherwise, this could turn into black magic.

Do not be attached to the outcome of your practice either, because that's how it unfolded for me. I was innocently "by accident" attracting these specific people into my orbit when I was focused on their cards. This is how you open energetic portals using thought physics. Trust, allow, and explore innocently, like I did, without expecting the outcome, and see what happens. It's OK to hope for a result, but since this is physics using the power of the mind, it's all new territory. We must not become emotionally attached; otherwise, that emotion may mitigate the plan. However, it's OK to feel, appreciate, visualize, remember, or love that person you hope to hear from as you experiment with this. Tell yourself it's OK if they show up, and it's OK if they don't.

However, if you desire something as opposed to someone, do the same exercise and watch that thing show up in your life. I understand how this happens with people, but I don't fully grasp how it might happen with things yet, so the jury is still out on how long it might take for that "thing you desire" to appear. If it's a thing, without a birthday, of course, you would use the Star Code Letter Calculator on my website to track which card that thing vibrates to. For example, suppose you want a new fancy blender for your kitchen—type in the word Blender to find its card. I have found that using capitals for the first letter is the most accurate, but you may also track it with lowercase as a backup. If anyone feels compelled to research this further, please contact me because I would love to be part of the study group and results. So, you see, there are many ways to use this book besides following the steps below.

1. Go to the back of the book to look up your birthday and find your External and Internal cards.

Why Two Cards? External and Internal?

On the most mundane level, the human condition has two parts: The part of ourselves we show the world and the part we keep private. We are multidimensional Beings, unbounded and infinite. We are much more than our External and Internal cards, but learning about those cards is a good start. If having two cards confuses you, think about it this way: If your genetic makeup is 50 percent Italian and 50 percent French, and people ask about your heritage, what would you say? You are both. As searching online for one's ancestral heritage becomes more prolific, we discover people with over ten or more inherited cultures. We can study each culture's characteristics and genetic influences to understand and apply their innate attributes to ourselves. The same goes for the 52-Star Code System. We blend the Internal and External cards, find what resonates more and less, and discover our authentic selves. I can attest to the accuracy of the description of my Four of Hearts External card and my Six of Clubs Internal card. I have read about the other cards in the deck that do not describe me.

2. Go to the chapter(s) connected to your External and Internal cards to familiarize yourself with all the information. Feel free to explore all your layers by reading the associated chapters, as your External and Internal cards pages reveal. If you can't find someone's birthday, you might consider a membership to Mylife.com. It's affordable, and I have discovered many birthdays on this site and on Facebook.

Were you born within an hour of midnight?

Are You a Cusper? If you were born approximately 1 hour before or after midnight, you would reflect two Natal External cards and two Internal cards instead of one. Why? Because you may have one foot on one side of the midnight with an entirely different card. The other foot may be on the other side of midnight, reflecting yet another card. You may be straddling the mystical midnight hour when new codes begin, and old codes end. This midnight birthtime puts you in a unique category of Cuspers. If none of the information resonated with you on the birthday you identify with and you don't know what time of day or night you were born, you may have been born 1 hour before or after midnight and are looking at the wrong card for your birthday. Or, at least, partially wrong. Read the cards on the day before or after your birthday to see if they resonate instead. Read more about this in the "Are You A Cusper" Chapter.

3. After discovering all your other layers, like your stress card, healing card, and more, found in the chapters on your

External and Internal cards, complete the worksheet at the back of this book, listing your External and Internal cards and all the associated layers. All the different cards, aka codes, are known as the "Layers" that make us multi-dimensional, unbounded beings. You will find your Healing-in code, Healing-out code, Primordial code, and many more under your External card chapter. Putting all the Layers together to understand your story may initially feel intimidating. Think of yourself like one huge rainbow made from many different layers of color. Read the chapter called "All the Layers" for more information.

4. To predict your future or track your past using this 52-Star Code System, purchase Robert Lee Camp's software at 7thunders.com, join his affordable monthly membership, or visit my Star Code letter and birthday card calculator and other widgets on my website.

Is the 52-Star Code System Similar to Tarot?

The 52-Star Code System is unlike Tarot, although some overlap exists. Tarot cards are strategically placed in a specific spread, reflecting the consciousness and truth of the moment. A Tarot card reading might include another strategical spread laid out two minutes later, which may differ entirely from the first. This 52-Star Code System is rooted in astrology, math, science, sacred geometry, symbols, and archetypes and reveals our life blueprint. Your "Layers" are based on the mathematics of your birthday; Tarot cards were developed from the 52-Star Code System when it was outlawed eons ago. The gatekeepers of the 52-Star Code System found a way to keep some version of it alive, hidden in plain sight, disguised as a Tarot. Yet the differences are apparent. Tarot has its merit and is very credible, but in a different way.

Please Note

Some of the charts and graphs inside this book include abbreviations of the cards. Examples: JH = Jack of Hearts. 2D = Two of Diamonds. 4C = Four of Clubs. 5S = Five of Spades.

Are You a Cusper?

"At the midnight hour, I can feel your power." - Madonna

If you were born 1 hour before or after midnight, you fall in the Cusper category. They are a fascinating tribe—they often also 'family' together. I knew a family of 5 brothers, all born around midnight. Cuspers surround me in my family, though I am not a Cusper. My husband, daughter, mother, brother-in-law, and other family members were born around midnight.

I have discovered that Cuspers have a unique intuitive gift. Many Cuspers are highly psychic and have more complicated layers/codes than average, making them difficult to track and read. Before learning this, I was always perplexed as to why I could not read accurately for my daughter and mother but could read accurately for my clients. Frustrated, I was determined to figure out this puzzle. Nothing is by accident; I was born into a Cusper family, so I could understand and recognize them as an entirely different and separate species.

There is something magical about the midnight hour. Cuspers can choose which Star Code they want to play at any given time. Their choice evolves around the two cards they are playing. Today, I was chatting with my daughter about clarifying which card she wanted to reflect into the world since she is a Cusper. She was born at 11:29 pm, cusping the Ace of Diamonds and King of Clubs. {It's interesting that I was born on 11/29- November 29. Our birth times are certainly not random.} The Kingly side of her wants to be a single, powerhouse rockstar businesswoman with no kids or commitment. However, her Ace of Diamond's side would love to find a husband, provider, and protector and raise a family.

Now that I know my daughter is a Cusper, I can read her cards more accurately. The best way to read a Cusper is by rectifying her chart. Rectification involves tracking backward to see what layer she was most recently playing. It includes asking questions about her previous week or a few days prior. I will use that card as the most credible one as we advance. However, Cuspers can turn on a dime and seem to have split personalities. I often must open two charts for Cuspers and oscillate between the charts to find confluence and accuracy.

Another interesting phenomenon is that Cuspers live partly in another dimension or density within this Earth realm. Are they living in a parallel universe? I am still exploring this theory. I have developed a parallel lifetime formula and have tracked at least 11 clients living in parallel lifetimes with someone from this lifetime. Learn more about that in my 52 Star Code Student Guide. Is living in a parallel universe making them so psychic and sometimes ungrounded? While unraveling this Cusper mystery, I was guided to add their two Star Codes to get one Star Code and explore the accuracy. I have done this with innumerable Cuspers and found it incredibly insightful. That means my daughter would also play the Ace of Hearts External card and the Jack of Clubs Internal card in another parallel density, directly impacting this density.

Here's the math: Ace of Diamonds is 27, plus King of Clubs is 26. {27 + 26 = 53. Subtract 52 = 1 Ace of Hearts.} Then we add her Internal cards: Five of Diamonds 31 plus Six of Spades 45. {31 + 45 = 76. Subtract 52 = 24. Jack of Clubs is Star Code 24.} That would give her a Cusping Ace of Hearts with a Jack of Clubs.

Many folks dismiss this 52-Star-Code System because they are Cuspers and don't know it. Before I knew about Cuspers, I would have some clients, not many, come in for readings, and I just couldn't read them accurately and even questioned their birthdays or asked if they were adopted and given a wrong birthday. Some have felt slighted and upset and thought I was a gypsy, taking advantage of them because I wasn't able to "find" them and give them any accuracy. Thankfully, that doesn't happen anymore, but I had to learn the hard way. Now, when I sense I am reading for a hidden Cusper, I will explore the card of the day before or after.

> Anything that is not love is only a visitor to your body. You are not anxious; stress is simply flowing through you. You are not permanently depressed; sadness is simply visiting you. You are not lost; confusion is simply wandering within you. And you are not broken; pain is simply passing through you.
> -Tahlia Hunter

Genesis of the Suits: The Ankh

The ancient key representing birth, death and the mysteries inbetween.

The suits are sacred geometrical shapes that date back to the origin of the symbol of the Ankh. It is from the Ankh that the suits came into being. The Ankh is an ancient Egyptian symbol that symbolizes the many aspects of life, including physical life, eternal life, immortality, death, and reincarnation. The symbol is an inverted eye-shaped hoop with a junction directly below it representing east, west, and south, denoting the sun's path upward and over the horizon. The sound and letters of the Ankh are nearly identical to the first vowel and first consonant of the Sanskrit alphabet: "Ka" belongs to this group of gutturals: ka, kha, ga, gha, and ṅa emerge from "a." "Kha" is the second consonant. Sanskrit is the language of nature, dating back thousands of years. Perhaps it is around the same time the Annunaki gave humans the Ankh and the little unbound book of time, the deck of cards. The sounds of the Sanskrit language vibrationally heal and harmonize all of nature through sacred rituals and songs. It was never a language designed for commerce or regular communication. The Ankh symbol follows suit, embodying that same wonderment and mysticism.

Though its physical origins are uncertain, scholars believe it originated between the 30th to the 29th century BC. The Ankh meaning can also represent water, air, sun, and all elements required for life. Since the ankh symbol has been inscribed on stone coffins or sarcophagi, many believe it may also represent the union of heaven and earth. In addition, the ankh may depict a combination of the symbols for male and female, perhaps connoting the duality of this planet and the sexual union that leads to the creation of life. It has also been used as a key to open physical and ethereal doors to the secrets of life and schools of mystery. For all the reasons listed above, I inserted the Golden Ankh Symbol in the background of the Earth Template at the back of this book.

The suits represent the mental and emotional bodies, which are intrinsically dynamic. Suppose you are reading the cards for someone inquiring about another person, for example, their lover. Their lover's card can be tracked in the querent's chart, keeping in mind the suits of their lover's card are subject to change. Let's take a fictitious couple; for example, Tom wants to know if Ericka still loves him. Tom was born as the King of Clubs, so we open his King of Clubs chart to look for Ericka, born on a Three of Hearts day. Instead of seeing Ericka's Three of Hearts card in the typical planetary cycles that lovers would appear, like Venus, Neptune, or Pluto in Tom's chart, Ericka appeared in his Jupiter cycle (Jupiter governs money, not love) as the Three of Diamonds one week. The following week, she still reflects as the Three of Diamonds but in the more common lover's planetary cycles of Venus, Neptune, and Pluto. Why would she appear without her "heart suit so many times?" Why is she disguised in Diamond clothing? Your next question to Tom might be, "Is she after your money?" Are you financially supporting her?" Once you get the precise story, you can proceed more accurately with the rest of the reading.

We can't see the suits change in our charts while reading for ourselves. It's only through the eyes of another that we notice the changing of the suits. The charts of two people must be open simultaneously for this discovery. There must be an emotional or mental connection between those two people. The suits change depending on the emotional state of mind or mood. Suits are like clothing. We can alter our clothes just as we can adjust our mood. We can use the change of suits to understand how the querent feels or perceives the situation or other person, but again, we need two different people's charts open to make the observation clear. Suppose a person is born on a natal Eight of Diamonds day but shows up in the chart of someone she is dating as an Eight of Hearts in Mars one day. In that case, this may still reflect this Natal Eight of Diamonds person. Still, the Eight of Diamonds person may be perceived or intentionally appear as aggravated, emotional, or highly sexy as personified by the heart suit swap. This is the dynamic interplay and exchange of the suits. However, the root of the card, for example, the eight, remains static, no matter what.

Another example would be if you have an Ace of Spade's friend you borrowed money from and don't have the funds to pay her back just yet. You know she is getting impatient and wants the debt settled. Suppose she invites you to lunch on a particular day, and you wonder if she genuinely wants to socialize and enjoy your company or if she wants to settle the debt. If she shows up on that luncheon day in your 'card spread' as an Ace of Diamonds instead of her authentic Ace of Spades, you know she will ask you about "Diamonds," representing money. Knowing this ahead of time, you might want to avoid the awkward luncheon conversation and reschedule another day in your chart when she shows up authentically as her Ace of Spades.

Hearts

The Heart suit signifies acceptance, love, compassion, anger, sorrow, and harmony. Hearts are the second evolution of the ankh symbol, as represented by the two rounded corners and the genesis of the first actual suit. Hearts people love children, relationships, playfulness, and sex. They can emote deeper than the other suits. The Hearts are akin to the planet Venus, embodying all Her attributes, such as beauty, the arts, affection, marriage, divorce, opulence, the earth and water elements, and intimacy. The Queen of Hearts is the ultimate Venusian heart card. The hearts and diamonds have an innate female gender, representing the divine feminine, forming the shape of the breasts within its symbol.

Hearts are when humans learn about love, bonding, family, and how to master our emotional bodies. It signifies the timeframe of our childhood, representing babies, children, youthfulness, juiciness, vitality, emotion, and all matters of the heart, favorable and unfavorable. They never grow old inside and often age beautifully, keeping a youthful look. When one mixes water and earth, we get oily mud. One of my most outstanding teachers, Dr. Vasant Lad, told his class of about twenty-two Ayurveda students that Venus was the love planet and governed the oily qualities in the human body. Then, he mesmerized us all by telling us, "Love is oily." Well, of course, it is on all levels. It's messy fun!

Action: To Feel
Elements: Water & Earth
Direction: South
Season: Spring

Clubs

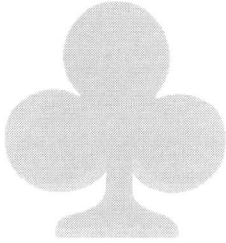

The Club suit signifies life's cerebral and intuitive areas, illuminating truth, understanding, mental and physical digestion, thought patterns, and brainiac ingenuity. In a broad stroke, this suit denotes the early-middle years of our lives as humans when we immerse ourselves in school. It's when we are most productive and accomplish our mission. They search for good conversation and communication and love to analyze thoughts, people, and situations. If they don't receive a gift, they might say, "It is the thought that counts." They don't miss a beat as they are detail-oriented people of the deck. Clubs denote our cerebral capacity and enjoy understanding the ethics between right and wrong. They make great lawyers, judges, and mediators and govern all litigation matters. They seek fairness and truth.

The clubs and the spades represent the male gender and genitals. They have incredible transformational mental digestion. Their internal fire helps burn away personal and collective outdated paradigms. As the great teachers of the deck, they teach us to make lemonade out of the lemons life throws us. Clubs are akin to the planet Mercury, which governs the intellect, discernment, consciousness, understanding, and communication, among other things. They are the third evolution of the suits from the Ankh, as represented by the three clovers, which gives rise to the four-pointed diamond suit.

Actions: To think and intuit
Elements: Fire & Water
Direction: West
Season: Summer

Diamonds

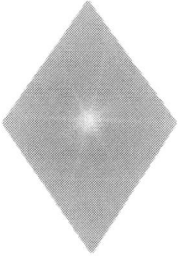

The Diamond suit signifies the seeds we plant on the Earth during our late to mid-life, hoping they will blossom into the wisdom of the Spade's suit. Diamonds are one of the hardest naturally occurring materials on Earth. They are immune to being spun upside, like the other suits. When spun, they remain the same inside time and space. Diamonds are the container for all the suits, starting with the Ankh. When we measure the letters in the word Diamond, its sum is Star Code 34, the Eight of Diamonds, the most potent card governing the entire deck. Like the shape of a diamond, the number Eight is also immune to being spun upside down.

Symbolically, Diamonds represent money, values, and measurable consciousness. It is also associated with the divine feminine and the shape of the birth canal and our beloved Mother Earth. In our mid-late years of being human, we developed newly upgraded value systems based on what worked and what didn't work in the past. It is when humans hopefully learn to take accountability for their actions and lives. Diamond people appear to be born "all grown up" and like to hang out with grown-ups and older children. The Diamonds are akin to the planet Jupiter. Jupiter governs the money (diamonds), principles, morals, values, and spiritual integrity. Sanskrit defines Jupiter as the Guru who dispels the darkness. Diamonds are bright and allow fractures of light inside like prisms. They are natural masters at managing all sorts of financial endeavors. The diamond person searches for personal value in the world by accumulating material things and money. They may even view their friends as an asset or a debt. They are natural masters at managing all sorts of financial endeavors.

Being born on an External and Internal Diamond suit day occupying the Earth Template's Jupiter row is akin to having a 'Maha Lakshmi Yoga' in your Vedic astrology chart—that type of yoga yields billionaires—causing money to grow on trees for them. Yoga means union, so I am referring to the union of Jupiter and Diamonds. Jupiter is one of the most abundantly massive planets in the galaxy and governs the earth and water elements, according to Ayurvedic medicine. During this time, we accumulate integrity and money as a nest egg for the Spades season, the Winter of our lives.

Actions: To measure and quantify
Elements: Ether & Air
Direction: North
Season: Fall

Spades

The Spade suit is a culmination of all the suits, so anyone born on a Spade Day may be considered an "old soul" or "wise being." I have noticed Spade babies look like cute little, wise older people from birth. They are born with innate wisdom, while the club's people thirst for knowledge. The Spade suit interfaces with the planet Saturn, who is considered the Great Sage Elder of the tribe of planets in the cosmos. Saturn resembles a disciplined, slow, steady, mature, and tenacious older adult. They are the worker bees of the deck and prefer "doing" instead of feeling, thinking, or evaluating. Often, they enjoy blue-collar work with their hands and tend to put work first. They strive for self-realization through accomplishments and their work.

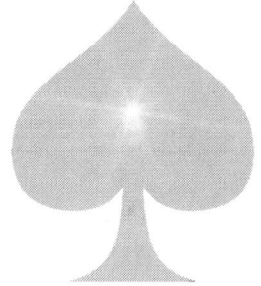

The Spade suit has an innate male gender and symbolizes the physical body regarding its structure, bones, form, and health. It has the essence of dryness in many ways, such as when we say, "Cut and dry," indicating firm boundaries. It may also mean dryness as opposed to hydration. As we age, by default, we dehydrate if we don't take precautions to reverse that.

This dry quality is vital to recognize when it comes to understanding the difference between the appearance of the Queen of Hearts and the Queen of Spades in our card spreads, for example. Why would one show up instead of the other? For example, the Queen of Hearts represents a robust, ripe, young, and juicy mother. The Queen of Spades may indicate an elderly lady, a grandmother-type, or a miscarriage in the Vertical placement. At the same time, the Queen of Hearts accompanies it in the Direct placement above it. Or it may represent a mother who needs care or who has passed or is about to pass.

In some cases, the Spade suit may indicate the final stage of something or someone and may give rise to health conditions. (Learn more about the placements in my 52 Star Code Student Guide). However, there must be confluence with other cards in the spread before any prediction becomes credible. We look to the Spade suit and the planet Saturn to give us messages about our health and life lessons. The Spades are the ultimate expression of Godliness and enlightenment by making lemonade from life's lemons. The Spade suit forms an upside Heart, and the cycle continues back to the heart suit, just as the Sun rises and sets each day. The Hearts and Spades represent the circle of life and are intimately connected. To understand this concept deeply, compare birth and death. They have a symbolic exchange in many ways, as the root and crown chakras are energetically tied.

Actions: Delay, dry, end, lesson, work, karma
Elements: All
Direction: East
Season: Winter

"He created His Universe by three forms of expression: Numbers, Letters, and Words." - The Book of Formation

Evolution of the Suits

The Tao gives birth to One. One gives birth to
Two. Two gives birth to Three. Three gives birth
to all things. — Tao Te Ching

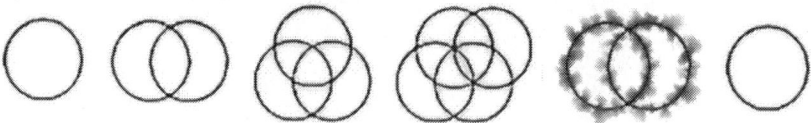

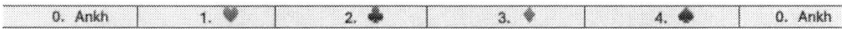

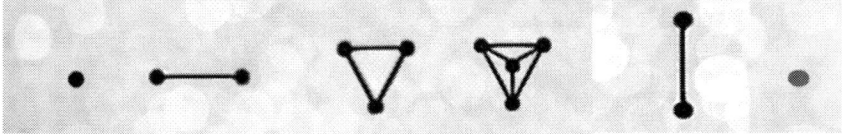

The Heart cycle represents babies and our youth. It is the Kapha stage of life, according to the science Ayurveda. The Club cycle represents when we go to school to learn, study, and discover our soul purpose to fulfill our soul contracts and serve the world when we graduate. This is the early Pitta stage of life, according to Ayurveda. The diamond cycle is when we begin serving the world with all the knowledge we gleaned during the club's cycle, collecting diamonds (money) so we can afford to live away from our parents and become autonomous. This is the later Pitta stage of life, according to Ayurveda. Then, humanity reaches the Winter of its existence, which Ayurveda calls the Vata stage; it is represented by the Spades suit. This is when our bodies begin to dehydrate, atrophy, and wither. Yet, it is the wisest, most liberating cycle of all as we review our lives, live in gratitude, and prepare to return to the Heart cycle, perpetuating the circle of life.

Star Code Terminology

What we know is a drop. What we don't know is
an ocean. - Isaac Newton

Using the term "Star Codes" is a more concise and descriptive
way of saying the word card. I will use the words "code" and
"card" interchangeably throughout this book. They mean the
same thing here. Also, I may use the words "harmonic" and
"vibration" interchangeably, referring to cards and codes
because cards are hidden codes that give rise to a measurable
vibration, creating a star language that gives rise to sacred
sounds, frequencies, and harmonics.

External Cards

I AM
External Card = I
Internal Card = AM

For brevity reasons, I may interchangeably use the words Natal,
Birth, Sun, and External in this book. They refer to the same
card. Despite its many names throughout many card schools

and books, we can discover this card by examining the month and day we are born, not the year. I coined the descriptive word "External" because this card is often how the world sees us. It's visible, like the Sun. In astrology, the Sun represents the self and the soul. The External card represents the "I" in "I AM." The letter "I" exchanges with the Nine of Diamonds Star Code 35. Please refer to the Letter Value Key at the back of the book. The Nine of Diamonds represents the end of something valued. Perhaps what was valued was our true essence while we were in unity consciousness, where we were all one.

Incarnating means we buy into the illusion that we are separate as we journey to remember we are never separate. What a wild ride! When we add the "I" (Nine of Diamonds Star Code 35) to the "AM" (Ace of Clubs Star Code 14), we get the Ten of Spades Star Code 49. (35 + 14 = 49.) The Ten of Spades has reciprocity with the Ace of Spades card, representing the mysteries between life and death and the entire deck. The Ten of Spades is the spiritualized version of the Ace of Spades. Please read more about that in the Ace-Ten Exchange Chapter of this book. The Zero is everything and nothing, the alpha and omega, the space between the inhale and exhale and the sunrise and sunset between the day and the night. It is the sacred pause before we make a massive decision and the transcendental state we can reach during silent meditation. Also, the Ace of Clubs's Primordial card is the Nine of Diamonds, representing the essence of the Ace of Clubs and the sacred union of God and Self, the I AM. God is the essence of All That Is. Notice the zero in the word God.

Life is but a dream. In truth, there is no "I" if we are all one, but while we are on Earth, we agreed to play the charade so we could remember who we are by learning more about love in a world of duality. The "AM" corresponds with our Internal card, also known in other systems and books as the Planetary Ruling

Card. The letters in "AM" add to 14– the Ace of Clubs Star Code 14, indicating the incarnation into sovereignty in the sacred present moment. This number 14 applies to the lower and upper case "AM." It aligns with the meaning of Source, God, or whatever terminology suits you.

It can also be written in lowercase as "i am." It's less formal, indicating humility, which gives rise to perhaps less ego in a more awakened state. The lowercase "i" exchanges with the Nine of Hearts, meaning an emotional end of something cherished. It may denote the tears of delusion that veils the truth. Why? Because when we come to this planet, we agree to take on an ego, creating the illusion that we are separate from the Infinite Field of All Possibilities or God or whatever term you wish to use. An ego is necessary to function on Earth and fulfill our soul contracts. We must lose ourselves to find ourselves again. On the other hand, the Nine of Hearts is sometimes the biggest blessing ever and a dream come true when it occupies a Jupiter cycle.

When we add the "i" (Nine of Hearts Star Code 9) to the "am" (Ace of Clubs Star Code 14), we get the Ten of Clubs Star Code 23. Since Aces and Tens are reciprocal, the Ten of Clubs is also the Ace of Clubs with a Zero included (9 + 14 = 23). Adding the Zero to the "am" Ace of Clubs, forming the Ten of Clubs when we say "i am", reminds us that God is with us now, in us, and is us all at once. The Primordial card to the Ten of Clubs is the King of Hearts, the Loving Father. The 'I AM' is the inseparable union of you and Source.

The External card is the starting point for discovering your life path in the Earth Template, which can be found at the back of this book. Your External card's traits reflect the experience your soul came to explore in this lifetime. It reflects how you show up in the world. How do you show up? Your External card will tell us. However, in childhood, we may appear as one of our

Exaggerated cards because the "Self" hasn't been fully established. Children may oscillate between their authentic External card and one of the Exaggerated cards that belong to their External card.

Since we are an amalgam of many unbounded harmonics, layers, and multi-dimensional existences, this particular layer, the External layer, aka card, is what we project into the world, just as the Sun shines its rays on Earth. Your External card may be the first layer people see when they meet you. It may be the card you identify with in childhood. Use the birthday chart, which can be found at the back of this book, to discover your External card. You can learn about your other personal layers, cards, harmonics, and codes from there. They are all based on your External card. To sum this up, cards are mathematical harmonic codes that comprise all the layers within and around you that make you as unique as a human snowflake.

The birthday chart at the back of this book has its roots in the mystical calendar of time. It was created eons ago based on a secret mathematical quadratic formula reflecting the four seasons of our planet. If you prefer not to use the chart, here's another clever way to discover your External card: Take the number of the month and day you were born. Double the month, add the day, then subtract from 55. The remainder will be the Star Code of your External card. See the Star Code Letter Value Chart at the back of this book. Example: Suppose someone is born on January 2, depicted as 1 / 2. Next, double the month's number: 1 + 1 = 2. Add the day of the month (2) to your first total: 2 + 2 = 4. Next, subtract 55 from 4. (55 - 4 = 51). The Star Code is 51, the Queen of Spades, according to the Star Code Letter Value Chart at the back of the book. Result: Anyone born on January 2 will have an External card of the Queen of Spades.

> *The spiritual journey is not a career or a success story. It is a series of small humiliations of the false self that become more and more profound.* - Carl Jung

Internal Cards

This card reflects the patterns, traits, and characteristics we identify with after childhood when we discover who we are, separate from our family. It represents the "AM" in the "I AM." Read the paragraph above for more detail. Some systems call this the Planetary Ruling card. This card holds as much weight as the External card, but that varies according to each person. Of all the different layers, cards, codes, and terminology, the External and Internal cards will hold the most weight regarding making predictions and tracking time back and forth in this 3rd dimension. However, if your Decanate Ruling card is different than your Internal card, I have seen that it holds more weight than any card in some cases. Only some people are assigned a separate Decanate Ruling card compared to their Internal card. That is determined by the degree of the Sun when you were born. Find your Decanate Ruling card under the chapter of your External card.

According to tropical astrology, the Internal card is calculated by the planet that rules the sign of the zodiac you are born under. We live in a world of duality, which explains why we have two primary cards. I often relate more to my Six of Clubs Internal card than my Four of Hearts External card. Finding which of your layers suits you best is where free will comes into play. We get to choose which harmonic resonates best within our birthday and focus on that. Find your Internal card in the Birthday Chart at the back of the book.

Decanate Ruling Cards

These cards can help point people toward their best career path; however, I have found many other profound insights in this decanate layer. What we can glean from the decanate card will depend upon the individual and their ability or desire to keep work separate from their personal life. Some people blend work and personal life, while others have firm boundaries. Those who combine work and personal life will have a spectrum of insightful information in their Decanate Ruling card. Depending on the degree of the Sun at the time of birth, some people will or will not have a separate Decanate layer. Some people's Internal card will be the same as their Decanate card. Wiki says: "In astrology, a decan is the subdivision of a sign. To give a fuller interpretation of the zodiac signs, ancient astrologers subdivided each sign into approximately ten-day periods." Find your Decanate Ruling card in the chapter under your Natal card, aka External card.

Mirror Cards

We are all mirrors of and for each other. Other schools call this card a Second Karma Card. When we encounter people born on one of our Mirror card days, or if they have an Internal or Decanate card that is your Mirror card, these people are part of our timeless soul tribe. They may be the most profound mirrors of you. Somehow, they always find you. Meeting your-self in the eyes of someone who embodies your Mirror card can be an "ah-ha" moment inspired by an elusive memory of a familiar sweetness. You would be at the receiving end of the directional flow of sweetness between you and your Mirror card. When your Mirror card people accept this directional flow and are grateful to meet you, they can play their role of returning favors to you. This can be a harmonious exchange, but there is no guarantee because their other cards (Internal, Primordial, Shadow, Decanate, or Imprint) may mitigate this. If so, this may cause an intensely bittersweet taste between you. However, this exchange depends on the person's awareness levels and maturity. Find your Mirror card in the chapter under your Natal card.

Our Mirror cards, and all cards, are not limited to the embodiment of a person. This card represents a harmonic with a favorable karmic undertone in most cases. When we meet people who embody our Mirror card, it is their free will whether they wish to step up and do any favors for you. However, they may feel magnetically drawn to you unexplainably if they are in the flow of grace. These harmonics stem from another lifetime where you earned good merits in association with all people, places, events, composites, and things vibrating at your Mirror card's mathematical frequency. The harmonic owes you in this lifetime, not the person or the soul.

I have had several friendships and relationships with my Mirror card over the past two decades. One of them was young, intrinsically selfish, and failed to step up and act like a genuine Mirror card to me. However, her Internal card was my Natal Pluto in my Lifepath, leading to the bittersweetness. She was greedy and wasn't in the flow of grace, but we still got along famously because I decided to lower my standards and accept her for where she was. It was through understanding her that I could soften and transcend the pinch.

Another one of my "Mirror card people" was young and immature with emotional disturbances. She was potentially a sociopath, unstable, teary-eyed genius. She drained me because she couldn't be authentic to herself, never mind to me. I could not even track which card she played when she came for readings. She was elusive, not operating from her authentic External card, even when I rectified her card spreads. I had to let that friendship go even though she was my Mirror card.

Another person who embodied my Mirror card was a student in one of my classes when I lived in Fairfield, IA. Though we didn't know one another except during the 2-day Sacred Stone Therapy class I taught, she was emotionally mature, kind, and a skilled meditator. She gifted me with one of the best gifts I could ever imagine. I didn't ask for this gift and never knew it existed. A week after class, she knocked on my door with a box of semi-precious stones embedded inside lights for chakra gemstone therapy. She said she used them to heal her son's incurable disease and didn't want them sitting in her closet anymore. She stated she could think of no one better than me to give these stones. Inside this treasure box was a natural pearl, diamond, emerald, ruby, tiger's eye, topaz, and so much more. Speechless, I hugged her with immense gratitude and have helped heal many people with them.

I have another dear friend I met around 2005. He was my Mirror and Pluto card combined, which made it an interesting bittersweet connection. We were comfortable with one another immediately and became fast friends. We started collaborating in the massage industry, selling products together. I could feel the push-pull between my Pluto card and my Mirror card. The intensity from Pluto superseded the sweetness on some days and vice versa on other days. We are still friends, and I am grateful for him in my life. Find your Mirror card in the chapter under your External card.

Shadow Cards

Everyone is assigned at least one Shadow card, which is determined by the Natal card. This card represents a harmonic with an unfavorable karmic undertone in most cases. How this plays out will depend upon the free will and consciousness of the person who embodies your Shadow card. These people belong to our soul tribe; we have been incarnating with them forever. By default, they illuminate and ignite the shadowy parts of ourselves, giving us the opportunity for spiritual growth. The directional flow between you and your Shadow card goes from you to them. There is a karmic debt from another lifetime. This can be a harmonious exchange, but there is no guarantee because their other cards (Internal, Primordial, Shadow, Decanate, or Imprint) may mitigate this. If so, this may cause an intensely bittersweet taste between you.

> *We don't fall in love with people because they are good people. We fall in love with people whose shadows we are familiar with. We can fall in love with someone for all the right reasons, but that doesn't guarantee success. When we fall in love with a person because our shadows perceive them as home, where they evoke patterns played out in our immediate families, that's the type of love where skin chemistry takes over, and they own a piece of your soul. Love is found in the shadows just as a candle lights the darkness. In my 22 years of advising with the cards, I have observed about 75 percent of my clients married to their shadow cards. It may not be ideal, but those are "our" people, our soul tribe with whom we "fall" in love and marry. - Karyn Chabot Martino*

Our Shadow cards, and all cards, are not limited to the embodiment of a person. Since cards are frequencies, they can be tracked within a place, event, composite, or thing when we measure the letters associated with that place, event, composite, or thing. For example, this applies to the spirit of the land, names of organizations, events, and Star Code composites. Living on a property with the same harmonic as your Shadow card might mean you did something unkind to that land in another lifetime and have returned to heal the land to repay your debt. For example, if you were born as an External Queen of Hearts and bought land on Park Ave. When we add the letters of Park Ave up, it comes to 22, the Nine of Clubs. All Queen of Hearts have a Shadow card of the Nine of Clubs. That purchase may indicate your soul is ready to pay a debt to that land. You could heal the land with sacred ceremonies, for example. Or are you married to your Shadow card? The energetic directional flow would move from you to your spouse. Your spouse would be at the receiving end, causing you to feel subtly drained. However, if you are also your spouse's Shadow card, that could mitigate things. Such a dynamic might make matters dramatically worse. Each case will be different.

This news doesn't mean you should avoid your Shadow cards; instead, use caution. Wayne Dyer once used a funny expression that is very fitting: "Sometimes, our soulmates are like "unflushable turds." Understanding this principle can help you rise above the adversities. Sometimes, understanding is more important than forgiving. Once we understand, forgiveness is just around the corner. Read more about the Ho'oponopono and forgiveness solutions at the back of this book.

My father and I create a composite of the Four of Spades, my Shadow card, and his blessed card. The relationship is much easier for him than for me. Our immediate family members embody our Shadow, Primordial, Stress, Blessed, and Mirror cards. They are our soul family, and we are back on the wheel of karma for another chance to do things right with them. I married my Shadow card and can attest first-hand to the directional flow. However, I am also my husband's Stress card, and we form a Neptunian Dirty Double Stargate of Black Sixes. Not easy, but there is love.

My Four of Spades Shadow card also represents health and real estate, among other things, not just for me but everyone. Having the Four of Spades as my Shadow card has contributed to my frequent moving, inability to settle in one spot, and some health challenges to overcome. Find your Shadow card in the chapter under your External card.

Primordial Cards

Below is the definition of Primordial from the Cambridge University Press: "Existing at or since the beginning of the Universe." It has no beginning or end, representing the infinite circle of life existing in and outside of time. Primordial cards denote the harmonic essence of every Star Code in the deck. What do I mean by essence? A rose is tangible. It occupies space and time and has a measurable harmonic, just like a card. However, its essence is the essential oil or the aroma of the rose. The essence is the most subtle aspect of anything, refer-ring to the spirit of each code as it exists outside of time and space. The cards may not have an aroma or essential oil like a rose, but each card is a code with an essence, a detectable vibration.

The Primordial cards may reveal deeply hidden quantum soul entanglements between people who have been incar-nating over and over together, learning about love and forgive-ness repeatedly. How is this knowledge valuable in a practical way? It explains why some relationships are so disconnected it feels as if the other is speaking another language and no one can agree. It may also explain deeply loving bonds between people who seemingly have no apparent compatibility but have a Primordial card exchange. It seems the Primordial cards are either very hot or very cold when we try to understand complex relationships with one another—nothing in between.

The information about the Primordial layer is still in its infancy. As I continue to learn more about it, I welcome all constructive feedback and ideas. I have seen people have horrible arguments and irreparable separations with their Primordial cards. Perhaps these are people we are also living in parallel lives with, in other dimensions, and can't seem to connect in this lifetime on this planet's frequency. I have also seen the Primordial cards play out beautifully between best friends, spouses, and family members.

The King of Clubs is Primordial to my Internal Six of Clubs card. My daughter cusps the Ace of Diamonds and King of Clubs. I see many Primordial connections in immediate families. I almost married a King of Clubs, but he died when he was 33. I was 36. He was one of my true soul mates whom I affectionately called Bear. He called me Birdy. I am 60, and as I write this book, Bear still visits me in Spirit frequently. Even though he has passed, I can still track him on the days he visits me in Spirit in my card spreads as the King of Clubs.

My father married my mother, who is his Primordial card. He was born as a King of Diamonds. The Jack of Diamonds is his Primordial card, my Mother's External card. His second wife, whose Primordial card is the King of Diamonds, was born on a Seven of Clubs Day. I am the Primordial card to my sister, who was born on a Four of Diamonds Day, April 17th. However, sadly, my sister and I are not on speaking terms. It's almost as if we don't speak the same language and can't understand one another. However, I have a college best friend who was born on a Four of Diamonds Day, and we are soul sisters for life. Again, there are no lukewarm neutral Primordial card relationships. Discover who the Primordials are in your life, and you will notice the extremes. We love or hate them, but remember, love and hate live on the same street.

I have also noticed that dying people will appear as their Primordial card in their last days on Earth. I have spoken to many hospice nurses who say folks who are on the edge of death will often talk to their loved ones who have passed on as if they are right there in the room with them—-and they are. They have one foot in this world and another in the other world. If you track them in your spread, they may appear as their Primordial card. I predicted my 102-year-old grandmother's death using the Primordials. Her External card was the Ace of Clubs, but she appeared as the Nine of Diamonds in my yearly Venus cycle, which was the time of her death. The Nine of Diamonds is the Primordial card to the Ace of Clubs. She also appeared as the Nine of Diamonds in Pluto in my cards on the week of her death and again on the day of her funeral. Pluto is a planet of death-like transformations where we can usually find the cards of people who have either passed away or caused us some trouble. Or, a card occupying your Pluto may indicate the transformation you might experience. Learn more about this in my 52 Star Code Student Guide. Find your Primordial card in the chapter under your External card.

Stress Cards

This is one of the most challenging cards in the deck. This harmonic can make us sick if we don't find a way to channel the frustration into something positive. If we let the stress get out of hand, it ultimately can become our demise and destroy us. I have tracked Stress cards appearing somewhere in the weekly spread of people who died, if not smack dab on the day of their death. Oddly enough, when we first meet people who embody our Stress card, we may deeply adore them. Indeed, they are part of our soul tribe. However, if and when the relationship turns sour, it can be earth-shattering. Somehow, they seem to have an edge over us, and we can feel helpless and defeated. This doesn't mean we should avoid them, but we should keep our eyes wide open and deeply understand the relationship dynamics.

In stress card relationships, I have noticed that the person reflecting the stress card to the other may feel compelled to act out of character, saying things they regret. They get all twisted up and tongue-tied. This makes matters even worse. It becomes exaggerated when the stress card person is an empath because empaths feel everyone's stress. The empath may perceive the other "like" a stress card simply because they feel the stress perceived by the other and react in an "off" way because they are at a loss for how to soften the situation.

I know a daughter whose mother was simultaneously her Stress and Pluto card. The mother was thrilled to have this Stress information because it removed the shame and blame between them. It gave her a new perspective. She always knew she was a good mother, but what defines a good mother is often the beholder's perception. The daughter's perceptions were clouded by the frequencies of her Stress and Pluto card when she would think about her mother or be in her presence. The stress prevented her from understanding and seeing her mother for who she was authentically.

With this new knowledge about the Stress and Pluo cards, which explained the soul contract between them, suddenly, the sad emotions and disappointment morph into math, science, fate, understanding, and forgiveness—in that order. Her daughter understands her mother better now that she explained this to her, too. It has mysteriously healed them but is still a "work in progress." Even our "Stress Card People" can be perceived as less stressful in the sunlight of awareness. Read more about the Ho'oponopono and forgiveness solutions at the back of this book.

I find at least one Stress card relationship in every immediate family. We end up "family-ing" with these folks because they have been part of our soul family from the beginning of time. Stress cards can also be hidden between family members inside the Star Code composites. For example, I have a brother-like friend in a very stressful twenty-year relationship with someone with whom he creates a composite of his Stress card. In other words, his girlfriend does not embody his stress card, but together, they form his stress star code, causing him to act out of character and all twisted up. This dynamic is tricky because the stress isn't coming directly from her. Instead, it's the relationship itself that is killer! This example is another case of the "unflushable turd syndrome" giving rise to love-hate relationships.

I have tracked the Stress cards in many families, but here is an example of how they played out in mine: I am the Stress card to my daughter. My Grandmother was the Stress card to her daughter (my mother). My father is my Stress card. My mother is my Primordial Stress card. (I find the Primordial Stress cards to be the toughest!) My mother is also the Primordial stress card to her stepson. They haven't talked in years. I am my husband's Stress card. My mother is the Stress card to one of my sisters, and the Primordial Stress card to my other sister. My sister's husband is the Stress card to my father. They hated each other at first sight, and he refused to attend her wedding. The saga continues.

I used to think I had the only crazy family, filled with Stress card connections, but I have been tracking this same "madness" in most of the families of my clients. This "madness" may be why family holiday gatherings can be stressful sometimes. The good news is, when you meet your "Stress Card People" who aren't immediate family members, and you like them, you can know that you have been family in many other lifetimes. They are our soul people. We must keep loving and forgiving them or do this repeatedly, lifetime after lifetime, in different clothing.

> *Thank you for the tragedy. I need it for my art. - Kurt Cobain*

Remember that the people who embody your Stress card are extensions of you. Please do not use them as an excuse or a way to escape accountability because that will only interfere with your evolution, and you may end up shooting yourself in the foot. Greet each Stress card person who shows up in your life with gratitude while your eyes are wide open, recognizing them as part of your soul tribe. The way to alchemize a soulless world into a sacred world is to treat everyone as if they are sacred until the sacred in them remembers. This isn't easy if someone has disrespected you, but if we remember that life is but a dream and that we are the dreamers, we can dream our lives into whatever we wish.

If you need guidance on forgiving, start with the Ho'oponopono Forgiveness Novena. For more information, refer to the chapter in this book titled Ho'oponopono Forgiveness. Find your Stress card in the chapter under your External card, or visit my website for the Card Calculator.

Blessed Cards

I discovered my Blessed card about eleven years ago after noticing the many people who have helped me out of the kindness of their hearts, especially when I needed it the most. Since then, I have discovered three more powerful Blessed cards for each birthday, but I will save those for my next book. Our "Blessed Card People" reflect more of you back at yourself in the sweetest way. The Blessed cards are you– exponentially. You are the blessing, but these people mirror it back to you with kindness. The kinder you are, the kinder your Blessed cards will be to you. I have found many children to be the blessed cards of their parents, as in my case. My daughter was a double blessing because my fifth house of children in my Vedic astrology chart is debilitated. I was lucky to conceive at all! This doesn't mean it's been an easy parenting road —-she's a female King and a Double Diamond Cusper—and with our Stressed-Blessed relationship, there's never been a dull moment. My Mother and her husband are each other's Blessed cards. Their relationship inspires me. Their Star Code Composite is the Jack of Hearts, one of the best composites to make with a beloved.

One of my best friends was a double Ace of Diamonds, born August 12. Another double-diamond blessing! However, her Imprint card is a Two of Diamonds, the Mirror card to my Six of Clubs Internal card. Her second Internal card is the Seven of Clubs, my Sun card, and the Primordial card for my King of Diamond's Stress card. Sometimes, our Primordial Stress cards are more difficult than our regular Stress or Shadow cards. Her Seven of Clubs and Two of Diamond layers produced another special bittersweet friendship, but more sweet than bitter. She knew how much I wanted to buy Robert Lee Camp's card software, but I could not afford it in 2005. She bought it for me and surprised me with one of the best gifts of my life! I am still in awe. She did many beautiful things for me that I will never forget, although our friendship was hot and cold due to the bittersweetness of how our layers impacted each other. After decades of a beloved friendship, someone gossiped about me to her, convincing her I was a traitor. I tried hard to correct this gossip and save the friendship, but it was too late, sadly. To this day, I still have no idea who said what, except that her bruised heart ordered zero communication with me. Her Seven of Clubs (my Sun card and Primordial Stress card) and Two of Diamonds (my Mirror card) may have trumped the double blessing. I still have hope that one day, the truth will come out, and we will be friends again.

I opened the first state-approved private Ayurvedic massage school in Rhode Island, but I could not have done it without the help of a lawyer who would not let the state educational board bully me. I didn't know him well, but he believed in me and saw how the Board prevented me from launching my school. They were understaffed, underpaid, and didn't have the proper paperwork for a small potato school like mine. My private small school would require too much work for them, so they dismissed me, lost my folders, ignored my calls, and did all they could to make it impossible. One of the staff was clergy from a local college. She challenged my ethics because of her preconceived notion that every massage therapist was a disguised sex trafficker. Once my lawyer showed up, they had to cooperate. He was an Ace of Diamonds and held my hand through everything, Pro Bono! And no, there was no romance or anything fishy between us. His intentions were pure, and his actions were genuine while he stood by my side the entire year during the grueling approval process. I could never have afforded to pay him, and that school would never have opened without him.

Another blessed story unfolded at Goddard College when I was one semester away from a master's degree. My lead professor was my Shadow card, the Four of Spades. She couldn't stand me and did everything she could to exhaust me, challenge me, embarrass me, and ultimately shame me for living in Fairfield, IA, the land of Transcendental Meditation. She was convinced I was a cult member, which I was not. I just liked to meditate. There was nothing I could do or say to impress her.

However, she commended me for being so tenacious and meeting her challenges with such vigor. "A" for effort, but "no cigar" as she intended to teach me a hard lesson. Regardless, she was about to fail me when another professor noticed the injustice and stepped in. She agreed to be my lead professor instead, unsolicited, and passed me with flying colors! What? I graduated! She was an Ace of Diamonds. My hero! A miracle! I have many more stories like this, but I think I made my point. I have recently channeled two more Blessed card formulas that I am excited to share in the 52 Star Code Student Guide with my readers. Find your Blessed card in the chapter under your External card.

The Blessed Trumped the Stressed!

If you cannot reach one of your stress card people by phone or any other form of communication, perhaps due to mysterious interference, no matter how hard you try, consider yourself in a state of divine grace. You are protected from that stress frequency for at least a few hours or longer despite your efforts to contact them. My father is one of my Stress Card People. At 82 years of age, he is lonely and usually answers his phone when I call. This concept about a "divine block" between you and your stress card person came to me one day when I had my Blessed Code and other auspicious cards in my daily spread. I remember floating an octave higher than usual that day, infused with positivity, dancing on top of the world. It struck me that high-vibe harmonics playing out for me on this day from the powerful, blessed cards I had were blocking all stress frequencies from entering my life. They can't co-exist! It seems I had risen above them! The cards I had that day were a King of Spades in Venus (my Cosmic Reward), Ace of Diamonds (My Blessed card), Four of Diamonds (Secondary Blessed card), and a Subliminal King of Spades (Add the vertical and direct cards). It was quite a magical day! Learn more about the Secondary Blessed card and Subliminals in 52 Star Code Student Guide.

Blessed Cards in Unfavorable Planetary Cycles

When Blessed cards occupy unfavorable planetary cycles or pass through the 9 of Spades/6 of Spades portal, they may act more like your Stress code. Thank Goodness our Blessed cards rarely pass through that portal or occupy unfavorable planetary positions. They may act more like your Stress Code when they occupy unfavorable planetary cycles.

Your blessed Star Code may appear randomly, for example, as part of a license plate, price tag, clock, or phone number, where it jumps out at you. Don't search for it because then it's "forced." Blessings can't be forced. They usually appear out of nowhere under the good graces of light and love. Learn to distinguish such blessed moments by noticing goosebumps, chills, "knowings," or other body indicators. The body never lies. Consider that moment when you accidentally spot your blessed Star Code and all thoughts associated with it-a lucky moment. If you are trying to make a yes or no decision, consider "yes" when you spot your blessed code, whatever shape or form it takes.

Sometimes, we find ourselves torn between two similar items while shopping online. What's your ultimate deciding factor? Rock, paper, scissors? Heads or tails? Or what if one of the items has a price that matches your Blessed code? That's the one I'd choose! Or what if one has a price matching your Stress code? Choose the other item.

When Blessed Meets Stressed

Remember that when you meet your External Blessed card, that person's Internal card may also impact you, giving you a bitter-sweet or wondrous blessing. Or it may manifest the other way around, where that person's Internal card is your Blessed card, and their External card is your Stress card. Let us observe a male born on July 3. His External card would be a Queen of Diamonds, and his Internal card would be the Ace of Diamonds. Since this person is a male, his gender may cause his Queen to act like a King. That would make him a King of Diamonds in some cases, which is my stress card. His Internal card would be the Ace of Diamonds, my Blessed card. What then?

It's a mixed bag, sometimes favorable and sometimes unfavorable, but a highly significant person in your life. Someone who embodies your Stress card and your blessed card is someone you have most certainly known before, perhaps shared many lifetimes, and has agreed to show up in your life as both a gift and a challenge. However, the Queen of Diamonds, played out by a female, would not necessarily be perceived as my Stress card because it is the (male) King of Diamonds that is my actual Stress card.

Robert Lee Camp, author of Destiny Cards and many other fantastic card books, has this July 3rd birthday. He was one of my first and best teachers of this card system in the late 1990s. His teachings inspired me to write this book. He has played a significant role in my life, for which I am grateful. However, I can attest to feeling both the blessing and the stress of our relationship in equal proportion, which sometimes leaves me floundering.

My Internal card is the 6 of Clubs, part of the "Neptunian Dirty Double Stargate of Black Sixes." I extrapolate on these 8 Dirty Doubles in the Stargate chapter in this book. My 6 of

Clubs inadvertently ignites that Stargate, which can cause any Queen of Diamonds stress, male or female, because the Queen of Diamonds Stress Code is the 6 of Spade's Star Code 45 and is in cahoots with 6 of Clubs to create a Stargate. Remember, all Queen men may express through the 'King' of their suit from time to time and vice versa. Gratitude can supersede all incoherent feelings. With gratitude, forgiveness, and love, I openly thank Robert for all our other lives together, especially for bringing this knowledge to me again in this lifetime.

It might prove insightful and exciting for everyone to find the birthday that embodies their Blessed and Stress cards and note how significant, favorable, and unfavorable these people have been in their lives. Extend genuine gratitude and forgiveness, then watch the relationship soften.

Exaggerated Cards

These are harmonics, like the black keys of a piano, reverberating to a note that might be perceived as the sourer note of the white keys to the bottom left or right. However, only some people are sensitive enough to differentiate between the two unless you listen and observe. The black notes still belong to the white notes by association, giving the piano a more robust sound. We have all had moments in our lives where we may have acted on a sour note instead of our genuine self. Those are moments of what I call exaggerations of our authenticity. In Vedic astrology, we have terminology for this as well. We call these sour notes 'debilitations and exaltations' of the planets. The planets remain the same but may become the flat tires on our bus of life.

We track these exaggerations using the royal cards of our External suit. For example, an External Two of Diamonds person may appear as the Queen of Diamonds, her Exaggerated Self. If she is gender fluid, she may also appear as the Jack or King of Diamonds. The same goes for men. They will play out the Jack or King of their suit when expressed as their Exaggerated Self. Again, if they are gender fluid, they may appear as the Queen of their Natal External card.

This Exaggerated layer may also be where we may vibrationally find children and teenagers when we open their card charts. Why? Unfortunately, it's normal and natural for children to experience an identity crisis. Why is childhood naturally challenging? Childhood is when we are in our most potent time of self-discovery because it is when society programs children with disingenuous information. At the same time, these children undergo a blinding amnesia by incarnating into a planet ruled by "time." As time passes and children grow up, the concept of time causes us to forget. The more time that goes by concerning anything, the more likely humans will forget. This reflects the law of physics on this planet. Time is governed by Saturn, the planet responsible for helping us remember our true nature by inflicting the element of time. We are in a constant perpetual "re-membering" while here on Earth. We are born of love, but many religions say we are born of sin. This conundrum confuses children because they embody innocence, sweetness, bliss, and love. Babies are freshly born from the "other side," where unity consciousness is the religion.

Someone may have become stuck in their exaggerated self if there was a personal trauma or crisis in childhood or during their teenage years. This survival tactic is much like an alter ego. Until the trauma is healed, someone may enter adulthood in their exaggerated self and continue as such until there is a deep healing. It is up to the Reader to determine what card to read for someone, including ourselves. When the Reader does a technique called "rectification" and can't identify their client in their authentic self by going "backward in time" using significant events and dates, the Reader should track them backward using the rectification technique to find which layer of their exaggerated self has been adopted.

I once had a Three of Diamond's client who came for weekly readings for almost three years. I am very grateful to her because she inadvertently forced me to learn the true meaning of the Exaggerated cards and how to recognize the shifts and nuances that would make me know which card to read for her. She was in love with a yacht racer who was in love with the ocean. She wanted to know what he was thinking, where he was, and when they might have their next rendezvous. It brought her some temporary hope each week. She was lonely, desperate, bored, and extremely depressed despite her inherited wealth, talent, and beauty. On the days she would arrive for readings with a hang-over, hands shaking, and the lower lip extended, I would read her at her Exaggerated card, the Queen of Diamonds, for best accuracy because she was hung over.

I discovered this the hard way, however, because we both noticed my accuracy dwindled from nearly 90 percent to about 50 percent when she started heavily drinking alcohol while reading her authentic Three of Diamonds. She didn't associate this decline in accuracy with her drinking, but I did. I regret telling her this because she took offense. My intention was not to hurt her feelings but to illuminate the problem. Instead, I eventually lost her as a client, which was a blessing. The alcoholism worsened, and I kept finding her operating at her Queen of Diamonds when I would rectify her spread. Rectification means tracking backward, asking questions about what happened the previous week, and tracking who was involved.

We kept records of all her significant people and their cards to find them during rectification, which only took 5-10 minutes at the beginning of any reading. If none of what she reported happened in that previous week, that would be my clue to search her other layers and continue rectifying until we found what harmonic she was operating from.

The moral of the story: Drugs, alcohol, codependence, victimhood, righteousness, underlying phobias, and other incoherent emotions will lower our resonant frequency, pulling us out of our most authentic selves, represented by our External card. It can cause people to play from their Exaggerated cards if readers are not sensitive enough to observe these subtleties. It can also diminish the credibility of this profound 52-Star-Code system because reading someone at the wrong layer produces inaccurate predictions. It's akin to searching for life on Mars using the wrong lenses and claiming there is no life there.

What does it mean if my male client operates out of his Jack-exaggerated self compared to his King-exaggerated self? The Jack of any suit, when someone is playing that card but isn't authentically that card, indicates immaturity, escapism, shame, blame, victimhood, and ulterior motives. For example, suppose a 4 of Spades male is operating out of his Jack of Spades. His behaviors would reveal lying, stealing, cheating, blaming, or being a "Poor Me." Suppose a Four of Spade client was operating out of his King-exaggerated self. In that case, he might appear to be cocky, holier than thou, bragging, pompous, dictatorial, unforgiving, and righteous, indicating power struggles in his relationship and possibly with you, his "Reader."

The Royal Family

There is an intimate connection between the Exaggerated cards and the Royal cards. Vedic astrology has terminology for when a planet acts out royally or exaggeratedly. We call this 'acting out' as exalted and debilitated. Planets that act as exalted or debilitated are a little wonky extreme and may either become the flattest tire on your bus of life or your fullest tire. The word "exaggeration" describes both debilitations and exaltations, which I will use in this book. People born with exaggerated planets in their Vedic astrology charts usually have an External or Internal royal card or a card that occupies the crown line in the Earth Template. The bottom line is that the cards of the royal family may play out in the extreme. They may be profoundly powerful, successful, and wonderful people, or they may be unable to function in society easily. I have a friend who is a wizard with this 52-Star Code System. As part of his line of work, he visits many prisons. While there, he asks inmates for their birthdays, often just the day and month. Over the last two decades, he has noted that about 80 percent of prison inmates either have an External or Internal card in the royal family, occupy the crown line on the Earth Template, or are one of the three fixed cards: Eight of Clubs, King of Spades or Jack of Hearts. Why? Sometimes, the royal family can't follow the rules and has a "holier than thou" attitude. They march to the beat of their drum and write their own rules, even at the expense of their freedom, and end up in jail.

The royal family (Jacks, Queens, and Kings) usually have best friends, spouses, lovers, and family who are also in the royal family. They enjoy each other more than the rest of the "mere mortal" cards in the deck. I am half joking about mere mortals, but it seems to fit! Most commonly, Kings gravitate to other Kings. Kings and Jacks have a natural affinity for one another and often marry each other. However, the Jacks may be the only card to outfox the King. We can apply the principle: "Birds of a feather flock together." Male Queens may appear as the King of their suit when tracking them in someone else's spread. We can also read them from their King-Self to predict the future accurately. An authentic King may play his Jack-exaggerated self sometimes, so check for that. The same goes for female Kings or Jacks. For example, a Jack of Hearts female may appear as

Queen of Hearts in your spread. The same goes for a male Queen. He may emerge as the King of his suit when seen in someone else's spread. The royal family simulates exaltations—if you are an astrologer and understand how exalted planets operate in a chart.

Imprint Cards

Our Imprint cards represent flickers of significant memories from other lifetimes that carry over into our current lifetime, usually because something was unresolved or unforgiven, or there is a soul contract in place to bring a gift or something valuable into this life that was attained from another life. Imprints can be favorable or unfavorable or a blend of both. Each case will be unique. After much research, I have found Imprint cards to often be your External card(s) from another lifetime or some version of that card, like the Shadow, Mirror, or Exaggerated card of someone's External card. I have also observed the Imprint card as the card of someone you may have betrayed or killed in another lifetime and for whom you need forgiveness. Read more about the Ho'oponopono and forgiveness solutions at the back of this book.

For example, suppose you killed or betrayed an Ace of Clubs person in another lifetime. In that case, the laws of physics are configured such that by default, our Imprint card would be magnetized to seek forgiveness or make amends with that person in the next incarnation. In that case, your Imprint card may be the Shadow card of the person you betrayed or killed. For example, a Two of Hearts Imprint card may denote you murdered or betrayed someone who was an Ace of Clubs in another lifetime. Why? The Two of Hearts is the Shadow card (and twin card) of the Ace of Clubs.

There is no ethereal "Police" organizing who gets what

Imprint card or any card. Instead, all cards we are born into are a harmonic consequence of another incarnation or realm of consciousness. Imprint cards consist of emotionally magnetized invisible and measurable vibrational "cords" that function within the laws of physics on Earth. Such cords may appear like a massive cosmic spider's web, automatically connecting us to specific people and experiences. These divinely programmed cords work for us, helping us find where and to whom our cords are a mathematical fit so we may continue to learn more about love, forgiveness, and who we are.

Notice I don't say 'past' life because there is no time on the other side. Imprints can come from past, parallel, and future lives. Sometimes, our Imprint's Primordial card is the Natal card from your other lifetime—the one you carry into this lifetime. Check to see if it resonates. We have countless lifetimes, but we will carry over the imprints from the other lifetime that went unresolved, where we lost pieces of our souls from trauma, or when we developed an extraordinary gift we want to bring forth in this lifetime.

Instructions for the Imprint Card Formula: Add your External and Internal Star codes to calculate your Imprint card Layer. If the total is over 52, subtract 52.

Example: Birthday of Feb 24:
External card: Ace of Diamonds 27.
Internal card: Five of Diamonds 31.
27 + 31 = 58.
Subtract 52. 58 minus 52 = 6.
The card for Star code 6 is the Six of Hearts.

Six of Hearts is the Imprint card for February 24. Use the Star Code Letter Value Chart at the back of this to find the matching card. The Six of Hearts is the Mirror card to the Four of Clubs. The February 24th person may owe something to a Four of Club's person from another lifetime and has carried it over as an Imprint into this life. It indicates something unresolved from another lifetime. This is an example of a father-daughter relationship where the daughter's Imprint is the Six of Hearts, and her father was born on a Four of Club's day, the Mirror card to the Six of Hearts. This is called a *Quantum Entanglement*. Read more about that in my 52 Star Code Student Guide.

Imprint Star Code 6 Interpretations:

Unfavorable: She carries wounds from another lifetime concerning love, romance, relationships, peace of mind, and peace in her heart and may be working through what it takes to find balance, happiness, steadiness, and success in matters of the heart.

Favorable: She carries the skill set, happy memories, and the ability to create harmonious relationships in this lifetime due to her excellent choices from another lifetime. She is content and on the receiving end of stability in the emotional heart/mind complex.

How do we know if this Imprint will play out favorably or unfavorably in this case? We can know by inquiring directly and allowing the querent to tell us. Or we can look at her other cards to put the story together. Blending all the cards, as listed in the chapter "All the Layers," tells the entire story. Determining this involves intuition and connecting all the proverbial "dots" so that they take shape.

Do you have unexplainable talents or skills that you did not learn in this life? Many of us do. Were there things you just knew at a young age without explanation? The Imprint card explains the mysteries of childhood savants like Mozart. How did he learn to play the piano so brilliantly and at such a young age? Find your Imprint card in the Earth Template and study its life path, counting from right to left, starting with the card to the left of the card in question. In other words, count eight cards away, non-inclusive of the querent's card. Count eight away, moving from right to left. Use the order of the planets for this: 1. Mercury 2. Venus 3. Mars 4. Jupiter 5. Saturn 6. Uranus 7. Neptune 8. Pluto.

Example: To discover more about the Six of Hearts as an Imprint, External, Internal, or any card you want to learn more about. Go to the Earth Template at the back of this book and locate the Six of Hearts. It is located in the Mars row. Starting with the Four of Clubs, the first of the eight, as its Mercury card, continue counting, two of Diamonds as the Venus, Jack of Spades as the Mars, and so on, following the abovementioned order.

Another example for anyone with a 9 or 6 of any suit in their External or Internal cards is that you will get two Imprint cards when you flip the 9 or 6 upside down. In some cases, if you were born a double six or nine, you have brought four lifetimes into this lifetime as Imprint cards.

Example:
External card = 4 of Hearts Star Code 4.
Internal card = 6 of Clubs Star Code 19.
4 + 19 = 23
The Star Code 23 is a Ten of Clubs.

However, since there is a number 6 involved, we must

measure it spun upside to the 9 of the same suit = 9 of Clubs Star Code 22 to get a secondary lifetime we bring forth. The same goes for anyone with an Internal or External card of 9 or a 6. When you calculate this, keep this in mind because this may produce more than one Imprint card, which is even more insightful. The secondary lifetime imprint, in this case, would be 4 + 22 = 26, King of Clubs. In 2018, during an in-between sleep-wake state, I experienced a flash, or "download," of who the King of Clubs was to me in another lifetime; where I was born as an Ace of Clubs in Ireland on August 25, 1863. I was given his name, my name, and the story. I am writing another book on that, so stay tuned.

Meditating on your Imprint card may help you remember who you were in another life and what part of that life you bring to this life. The Imprint card resonates around you, just outside the veil of this 3-D world. Some experts use the term "densities," realms, or dimensions to describe this. Your Imprint's life path may give away the story of the lifetime that you carried with you into this life. You may even find some of the same people from that lifetime in this lifetime inside your Imprint card's life path.

Another way to understand the Imprint card is by studying how other cultures view the concept of reincarnation. The Sanskrit term 'Samskara' is akin to the definition of how I use the word "Imprint" in this book. Samskara impressions and dispositions develop and accumulate deep inside a person over many lifetimes. According to Vedic literature, Samskaras are from perceptions, inferences, choices, interactions with others, thoughts, intentions, and willful actions. Also, the phrase "Sins of the Forefathers" can be found in the bible with similar references and definitions. They are the energetic and emotional wounds from traumatic moments that were too overwhelming for the support and resources available in that lifetime. Hence,

Imprints follow us from other lifetimes for further integration and processing into this lifetime. These Samskaras manifest as tendencies, karmic impulses, phobias, ingenuities, subliminal impressions, habitual potencies, or innate dispositions. Search my website for your Imprint card if you have trouble with the calculations. I am developing a webpage where readers can use widgets to calculate their different cards, codes, and layers correctly.

As I said earlier in this book, the aces and tens of the same suit have an innate exchange. My Ten of Clubs Imprint represents the zero-ed out version of how my life ended in the 1800s as an Ace of Clubs woman. The man shown to me in a "download" from another life was born on a Queen of Clubs day, but he expressed himself through his exaggerated self, the King of Clubs. When he died in a mental asylum in the late 1800s, he got stuck in the astral realms, unable to find the light to "go home." Interestingly enough, the Healing-in card for the Queen of Clubs is the 4 of Spades. My Shadow and my First Name card are the Four of Spades. For some reason, I agreed to help him heal in a soul contract eons ago, despite the fact he murdered me in the 1800s and probably in many other lifetimes since each lifetime is almost a replica of our other lifetimes. Before I discovered he needed help "crossing over" to the light in 2018, he haunted me for nearly six months. The most significant indicator was that I smelled him everywhere, in ebbs and flows, and he would randomly knock small things over in my house to get attention. It was the scariest six months of my life. Now I know what it truly means to be haunted. The odor would come in wafts, like an elusive toxic wave I could not re-smell or grasp at will. Before I knew his name or the story, I called him the Poop Ghost. He was trapped in the astral realms for over a century. I forgave him and helped him get "home" with the assistance of six Shamans.

In 2018, when the Poop Ghost appeared, I was shown the lifetime where I was born as an Ace of Clubs External card and Queen of Clubs Internal card on August 25, 1863, in Limerick, Ireland. I didn't ask to be shown this and didn't want to know my past lives. I was more concerned with the present moment and my future and had no interest in going backward because I saw no value in it (little did I know). During that lifetime in the 1800s, I had the same birthday as my maternal grandmother in this lifetime which I still find fascinating. This is why tracking your soul genealogy through your Imprint card is so insightful. I stumbled upon this information during an out-of-body experience early in the morning before waking. I met an unidentified older female in Spirit who gave me his last name, showed me his death certificate, and gave me the necessary details to fulfill my soul contract in this lifetime. I feel she knew I could help him. I believe she was his mother. To learn how to have out-of-body experiences, I highly recommend visiting the Monroe Institute in Virginia.

After this remarkable and revolutionary discovery in 2018, there were still some missing pieces to the story. A few of my talented, intuitive friends and I compiled the rest of the story from channeling, lucid dreams, and Wikipedia. My mother, a professional genealogist, found a photo of her (me) at age nineteen. Photos were rare back then, so I am grateful she found it. I wish I had more. I look just like her—same color hair, face and body type. Her story on Wikipedia is also very similar to my current life story. I am writing a book about that lifetime, as I write this book. I had unfinished business from that lifetime that I had to complete in this lifetime, which is why I was born with the Ten of Clubs Imprint as opposed to the Ace of Clubs, her genuine Natal card. Read more about this in the "Ace-Ten Exchange" chapter. The zero in the Ten meant I had been zeroed out in that lifetime and had to do a soul retrieval, among other things, to heal that incarnation and help and forgive the man who killed me. Watch for the book to learn the rest of the story. It's captivating, transformational, and eye-opening. Meditate on your Imprint card to remember the lifetime you carry into this one, or hire a trained past-life hypnotherapist. Look for the life path of your Imprint card in the Earth Template for more details about your other lifetimes.

Higher Octave Cards

> The moment you change your perception is the moment you rewrite your body's chemistry." Bruce H. Lipton

This is the card we evolve and morph into after we have made lemonade out of the lemons life has thrown us. The Higher Octave card is the Pluto card in our Lifepath in the Earth Template, found at the back of this book. We always have the choice to be accountable and evolve or remain a victim, shaming and blaming others for the fires we walk through. Holding onto our past is the riskiest choice we can make because when we cling to the past, we erase any chance that we can change our future. According to our External card, we evolve to our Pluto card–the eighth card in our Lifepath. Instead of allowing our Pluto card to continue getting the best of us, we take the bull by the horns and step into that harmonic. We become the bull.

When we do this, we become that harmonic and face our demons with love. Shamans do this by literally stepping into their assigned jaguars instead of asking their jaguars to help. Shamans shape-shift into jaguars. We don't have to shape-shift into our Pluto card, but we must walk through inevitable fires that force us to evolve upwards or sink into pity. The beauty of this is we can keep evolving up an octave, eight away from our External card, then again, eight away from that card, and so on. It is unending. We can continue rising many octaves, creating the opportunity for boundlessness into the infinite field of all possibilities! As a result, I can effectively and accurately read myself at my Pluto card level and make predictions accurately now. Anyone can do this if they have walked through the fire and survived the flames of purification. Where is the evidence? When clients show up for readings, their daily card spreads reveal one of my Pluto cards instead of my External or Internal cards about 70 percent of the time. My External Pluto card is the Eight of Diamonds. My Internal Pluto card is the Queen of Clubs. I operate from these cards almost more than my Internal and External birth cards, as reflected in my client's charts when they visit me for readings.

The caveat is that we can only know if we have evolved by gazing into the weekly spreads of those who love us or if you are a Reader, use your client's daily cards when they meet with you to see how you show up for them. We use the weekly spread because it's the easiest, most profound way to track this. Check "how" your loved ones perceive you when planning a meeting with them or seeing each other. A significant phone call together would also be a way to track this. If you live with this person, choose days when something meaningful happened between you. This evolution doesn't happen overnight, either. Some of you may have a baby toe into your Octave Higher Pluto Card one day. On another day, you may appear as your authentic External self, but don't give up. Keep tracking this in the spreads of those who care about you, and if you are successful, you will appear as your Octave Higher at least 70 percent of the time since no one is Buddha all the time.

In Vedic astrology, we use similar terminology for such an

evolution. We call it the ninth divisional harmonic chart, aka D-9. We are all assigned a ninth divisional harmonic chart, but it becomes more fully activated with emotional maturity and age. The D-9 is much like our Lifepath's Pluto card. It is also called the Spousal Chart. Interestingly enough, our spouses usually show up in our Pluto positions in our spreads, too. Maharishi once said, "We evolve the fastest through relationships."

Also, there are numerous testimonies of those who have had near-death experiences insisting that when they crossed over and were shown a 'movie' of their life, it was revealed through the eyes of those we have hurt and those we have loved, not our own eyes. This makes perfect sense. If our "life review" was experienced through our limited earthly perceptions alone, we might miss how our life impacted others while we were on Earth. The energetic ripples we create with our actions, inactions, words, emotions, and thoughts while we are incarnated on planet Earth can go unnoticed and even dismissed if the inter-pretation is only up to us. This technique eliminates twisted perceptions of sociopaths, for example, who are unable to feel feelings of remorse, sorrow, joy, and pain. They may only experi-ence the pain they inflicted on others by using this "Unity Consciousness" life review technique through the eyes of those they hurt.

Becoming Your Pluto Card

66 *It is said that a river trembles with fear before entering the sea. She looks back at the path she has traveled, from the peaks of mountains to the long winding road crossing forests and villages. And in front of her, she sees an ocean so vast that to enter there seems nothing more than to disap-pear forever. But there is no other way. The river*

cannot go back. Nobody can go back. To go back is impossible in existence. The river must take the risk of entering the ocean because fear will disappear only then. Because that's where the river will know it's not about disappearing into the sea but becoming the ocean. - Khalil Gibran

I elevated an octave higher from my Four of Hearts Natal card to the Eight of Diamonds; my body's chemistry entirely changed when I moved to 34 Catherine St in 2016. In the Earth Template at the back of this book, you can find the 4 of Hearts and count eight away, non-inclusive of the 4 of Hearts, from right to left. You will land on the Eight of Diamonds. We can do this with all the cards to find the Octave Higher card for the querent's card or any card in the Earth Template.

In retrospect, I had no idea I was elevating when I chose to live at this location. It wasn't even a twinkle in my eye. The only way I recognized this evolution was in hindsight. Star Code 34 is the Eight of Diamonds, the number of Catherine St in 2016. It wasn't the move itself that elevated me. I decided I deserved better and chose to take my power back, which is what the Eight of Diamonds card is all about– power. I finally decided I deserved to be first in my lover's life, not second-hand Rose. Being second-hand Rose was the adversity that 'Pluto-ed' me up an octave! It was so painful. Unfortunately, Pluto is usually associated with pain. I caught my boyfriend of 2 years, with whom I was sharing a home, cheating on me during the eclipse of 2016. Eclipses generally bring out secrets.

He was born on Sept 26 as the Jack of Hearts Natal card Star Code 11 and Nine of Spades External card Star Code 48, a captain in the Navy, groomed to be admiral. The woman he cheated on me with had the Natal card of the 9 of Clubs Star Code 22. Together, their Nines activated the Venusian Dirty

Double of Black Nine's Stargate in the Earth Template. They were Stargate partners, and I could not compete with that, nor did I want to. The Star Code behind that Stargate comes to the Eclipse card 5 of Club's Star Code 18. When we enter the letters found in "Catherine St" into my online Star Code Letter Value Widget, the letters added together equal 18, the 5 of Clubs Star Code. Each letter equals a numerical value, making it possible to add up entire words to discover what card they are associated with. Everything and everyone around us are reflections of our consciousness, our harmonics.

Backtracking this story, I had caught this Jack of Hearts boyfriend cheating on me the year before with another woman, but I chose to forgive him and hoped we could earn the trust back as time went on. I regret forgiving him because the spots on a leopard never change. When you enter the word "Cheat" into the Star Code Letter Widget, it comes to 11, the Star Code of the Jack of Hearts. This discovery doesn't mean every Jack of Heart person will cheat, but there certainly is a huge possibility.

His cheating forced me to dive deeper into learning the language of the cards even more so I could track him cheating again because I had become paranoid, and rightfully so. After I caught him during our first year together using this card system, I accused him of cheating again in our second year because I foresaw "their breakup" in his chart coming in the Fall of 2016 with an Eight of Diamond's woman. These cards appeared in his Venus Cycle, where the Nine of Hearts occupied the direct position, and the Eight of Diamonds occupied the vertical position. I surmised that he was going to experience a breakup with this alignment. It would most likely be with an Eight of Diamonds woman he was cheating on me with. Funnily enough, as the Fall arrived in 2016, I was the one who broke up with him during his Venus cycle. That Eight of Diamonds woman was me; I didn't even know it until hindsight! That was another indicator I had elevated from my Natal Four of Hearts to my Pluto card, the Eight of Diamonds.

All I could focus on was building my self-esteem and self-worth from the betrayal while moving out of his apartment, getting as far away from that Jack of Hearts as possible. I happily nested at my new property at 34 Catherine St without him, which mathematically confirmed my Pluto evolution in hindsight.

Jumping ahead to 2024, I have one foot in my next Octave Higher, the Ace of Spades. Count another eight away from the Eight of Diamonds in the Earth Template if you want to follow along. I am seeing glimmers of the Ace of Spades in some of my client's charts on the days they schedule a reading with me, but I am not 100 percent elevated there yet as I vacillate between the Four of Hearts, Eight of Diamonds, and now, partly the Ace of Spades. Again, I am using other people's charts to track this. We can't use our own chart and "dub ourselves in" as elevated. I am on the cusp of several beloved family members dying in 2024 and expect to go through many painful deaths and death-like experiences this year, which may propel me to step 100 percent into my next Pluto card, the Octave Higher landing on the Ace of Spades. It won't be easy, so I am bracing myself. Discover your Octave Higher card by tracking the Pluto card in your Natal Lifepath on the Earth Template at the back of this book. Remember to count eight away from your Natal card, excluding it, moving from right to left.

Healing-in Cards

This mathematical harmonic helps ignite the portal of healing for each of us. When this card appears, we can trust improvements in our health are imminent. Or, when someone who embodies this harmonic appears, yes, the portal is also ignited.

Even an address that vibrates to this harmonic will create the space for your healing. Of course, this isn't the only way to ignite a healing portal, as many paths up the mountain exist. However, this is one very potent path, always at your fingertips. We can't force our Healing-In card to appear inside our spreads, but we can reach out to people we know who embody this harmonic. One of my dear friends creates my Healing-in harmonic when we talk, think of one another, or get together. His Natal card is the Eight of Spades Star Code 47. When we add his 47 to my 4, it totals 51, the Queen of Spades, my Healing-in code. When I connect with him, I always feel better. I use the Healing-in card to help track when a sick client may finally recover.

Why not choose a day with your Healing-in card and Star Code as shown in your card spreads or one of the yearly birthdays of this card if you hope to have a successful surgical operation, pap smear, biopsy, or any medical test, massage, or healing endeavor? Finding a massage or physical therapist, counselor, healer, doctor, or piece of property who embodies this healing frequency would bring you outstanding results. Surround yourself with friends who embody this card and connect with them when you need healing. Be kind to them, bake them cookies, or bring them a lovely cup of tea to exonerate and propitiate the sacred connection.

Be careful not to fight or antagonize people whose External or Internal card is your Healing-in card because it may negatively affect your health. I once challenged a teacher who embodied my Healing-in card. I filed a PayPal dispute against her because she did something very unfair. Getting litigious or contentious takes a lot for me since it's not my nature, but injustice is one of my pet peeves. After I filed the dispute, the next day, I developed a frozen shoulder for the first time in my life. One week later, she won the dispute. In my surrender, my shoulder miraculously healed. I knew if I continued prosecuting her, my shoulder would worsen. Avoid litigating with anyone who embodies your Healing-in card if you can help it. It may make you sick. Find your Healing-in card under the chapter of your External card. I will disclose the details of this formula in my 52 Star Code Student Guide for those who like to learn.

> You can't heal people you love. You can't make choices for them. You can promise that they won't journey alone. You can loan them your map. But this trip is theirs. - Laura Jean Truman

Healing-out Cards

This mathematical harmonic helps ignite our Healing-in portals by igniting our innate abilities to heal others. We all have the power to heal, but our powers to 'send' healing to others become magnified when this card appears. Ideally, if you are in the healing arts industry, tracking what days or cycles your client might have your Healing-out card would be times of massively successful results. Even better, imagine you schedule a client on a day when your Healing-out card appears in your spread, and at the same time, her Healing-in card appears. That would be a magical day! Of course, our powers to heal in and out are always present, but the appearance of these harmonics in our spreads are times when those innate healing powers are enhanced.

The formula for finding these Healing-in and Healing-out cards was conceptualized and channeled by a dear and brilliant Jack of Club's friend, Annette Burke, to whom I will always be thankful for this profound insight. Find your Healing-out card under the chapter of your External card. I will also disclose this formula in my 52 Star Code Student Guide for those who like to learn.

All the Layers

The infinite vibratory levels, the dimensions of interconnectedness are without end. There is nothing independent. All beings and things are residents in your awareness. - Alex Grey

Below are the frequencies we were born into and follow us for life. They are static. Our blessed card is a magnified version of our most authentic self. We were born of love and blessings, not sin. We will always be the embodiment of love. The layers below are static and intrinsically part of us all the time. The first four cards listed below are our primary cards. Learn about the meanings of these cards/layers in the Star Code Terminology chapter.

- External Card
- Internal Card
- Decanate Card
- Imprint Card
- Shadow Card
- Mirror Card
- Primordial Card
- Blessed

Below are the transiting and rotating personal frequencies that can go dormant or enlivened through divine timing, fate, consciousness, prayer, and intention. They are dynamic. The name card layer can change if you change your name. We are not born of stress or sin; that portal isn't static. Life is partly about learning how to manage and manipulate stress to stay healthy. These cards are like transiting planets and are ignited by fate, divine timing, prayer, consciousness, and intention. They rotate like a wheel around us. Each portal will be more intense as it passes over the center of your head. However, they are always there somewhere in space for us to access with our thoughts, prayers, and intentions. If we do not use intention, thoughts, or prayers, by default and divine fate, they will move along the wheel, affecting us differently at different times, depending on where they are, as they dance in space around us. They live and transit within time and space and are part of our life's blueprint.

- Healing-in Card
- Healing-out Card
- Exaggerated Card
- Name Card
- Higher Octave Card
- Stress Card

There are many keys and notes on a piano, but there is only one piano. There are many spokes on a bicycle tire, but only one tire. There are many colors in a rainbow, but only one rainbow, sometimes a double rainbow! There are many chakras and marma points within our bodies, junctions of consciousness, but only one body. We are multi-dimensional beings with many layers, harmonics, lokas, colors, sacred geometrical patterns, and sheaths. Ayurvedic medicine calls these layers koshas. Alex Grey, a master artist, is renowned for his ability to paint, draw, sketch, and see these layers. Barbara Brennon's School of

Healing teaches us how to work with these layers similarly to how we would heal chakras.

Each layer described above connects the five elements from the densest to the most subtle. Please visit the image at the end of this chapter for a coherent visual of what I am describing. The black figure in the middle of all the layers is the densest, carrying the most weight, representing the Natal External card. As we move away from the black figure in the center, out to the periphery, the layers become more subtle, equally as powerful and insightful, denoting another density or dimension, giving us a clue as to who we were in another life, where we are from, why we are here, and where we are headed.

As described in this book, the other layers and cards act like portals or large gateways rotating around us, similar to a cosmic clock or a sundial. Sometimes, I've noticed the portals have a two-hour window as they position themselves over our heads, activating a unique portal for that short time. At other times, I have noticed they can last as long as 24 hours, starting around midnight each night. Some portals will last longer, too, especially if they are in your card spreads for 52-day cycles or longer.

This 52-Star Code System is rooted in astrology, math, science, sacred geometry, symbols, and archetypes. Your "Layers" are based on the mathematics of your birthday. These layers dance together in a symphony of colors, weaving a galactic web and describing the stories of our lives. They are all significant. How they are interpreted and perceived is where our intuition comes into play. Trust yourself and your intuition to know how these layers interface and how they play out for each person.

When I refer to card spreads or cards occupying a favorable or unfavorable planetary cycle, it is easy to see which planetary cycle they occupy in Robert Lee Camp's software. Thankfully, he developed this software program so that we don't have to count and track the process of reading cards manually. Before the technology era, the old way of reading cards involved tedious counting and tracking, using 90 templates and probably banana leaves. (See the screenshot of his software on this page.) You may purchase and install his software on your computer or join his monthly membership at 7thunders.com.

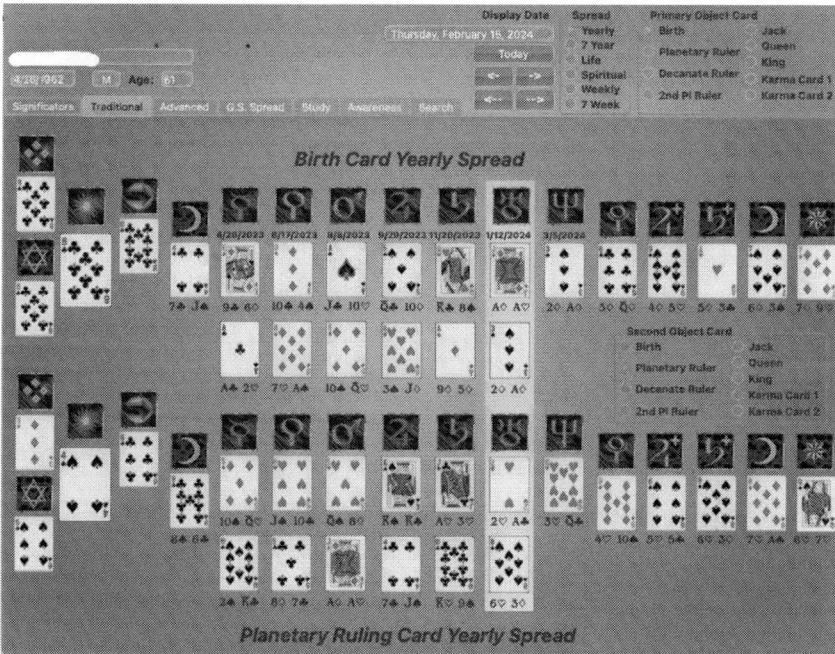

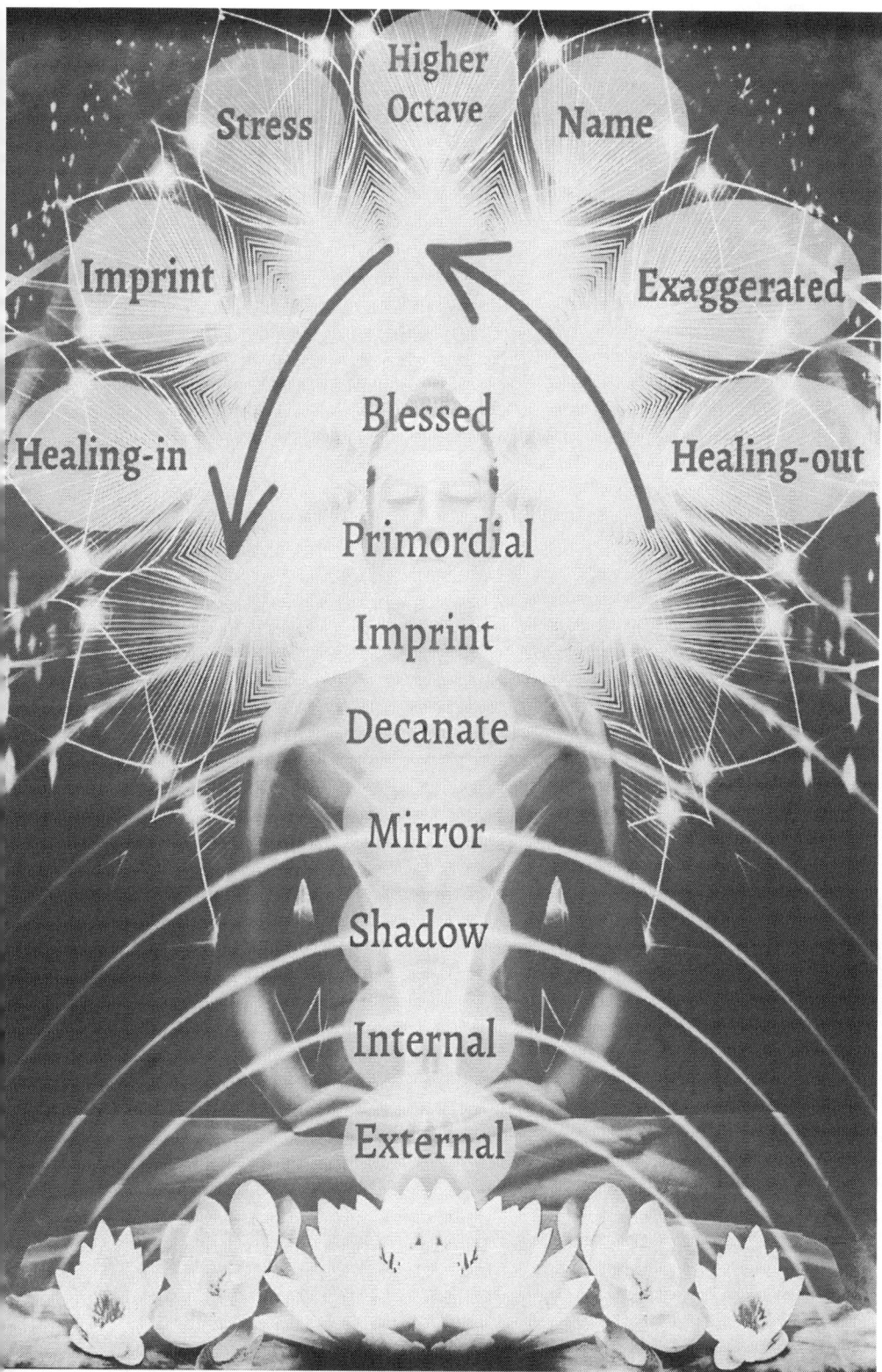

When a Card Appears

Nothing happens by chance.

A card may appear randomly by surprise on the street, or the Star Code of the card may show up on a license plate, an address, in our spreads, as a person, or some other way. Regardless of how it appears, it has a message for you. I know someone who prefers not to purchase card Software or open daily spreads but is a master at reading the Language of the Star Codes using his environment. Instead, he asks significant people around him, wherever he is, to disclose their birthdays, just the day and month, not the year, because that's all we need for this. They might be a waitress taking his order, a cashier at Walmart, a nurse in a clinic he visits, or a stranger at the bus stop. He has all the birthdays of the year memorized and knows immediately what that person's External and Internal card is. He compiles a list of all the birthdays of people he met that morning in his mind, along with the cards of street addresses he visited. He carries folded tiny papers in his back pocket listing the 90-card quadrations. That's how he predicts how the rest of his afternoon and evening will go. Maybe that's how cards were interpreted before the dawn of technology and card software.

When your Shadow or Stress card appears, its significations may unfold as if it's in an unfavorable planetary cycle, even if it's not. Our Shadow and Stress cards may always produce something uncomfortable when they surface, regardless of the planetary cycle. However, its pinch may be softer if it appears in a favorable planetary cycle. When your Blessed card appears in an unfavorable planetary cycle, your blessing may be entirely mitigated or watered down. It's not usually good when your Blessed card occupies an unfavorable planetary cycle, and your Stress and Shadow cards occupy unfavorable planetary cycles. However, the opposite can be true when your Blessed card appears or occupies a favorable planetary cycle, and there isn't a trace of your Shadow or Stress cards anywhere in that spread! Expect something extraordinary in that case!

How a card appears in the spread of someone who cares or is involved is one of the most insightful ways of understanding your relationship with them and how they perceive you. It's like wearing their moccasins for a moment in time. Our card spreads may also reflect the Star Code of a location, thing, name, or the composite between two or more people. The appearance of a card may also signify the Shadow or Primordial Code of someone important to you.

When analyzing card spreads, people don't always appear how you'd expect them to appear. People have many faces, traces, and layers. When you find a trace of someone significant in your spread, that particular trace or layer may reveal how they feel about you or the situation. For example, suppose they were born a 6 of Diamonds. Instead, if they appear in your spread as the 9 of Diamonds, it can mean they are not acting authentically or not feeling well, or perhaps they have an ulterior motive. Sometimes, when we only see traces of people in our spreads, which can take many disguises, it may indicate another past, present, or parallel life imprint is playing out. Or if they appear as their Shadow or Exaggerated card, you might guess there is unfinished business or a hidden agenda. How people appear in our card spreads depends on how we perceive them or how they choose to appear to us. Their appearance may reveal their feelings about you or a pertinent situation that involves you when their card or one of their faces, traces, or layers appears in our spread. The suits of the cards are considered clothing that represents how we feel. Just like we change our clothes daily, the suits can change when appearing in someone else's spread. Each suit represents the emotional scenery of a person, place, or thing.

For example, a Four of Diamonds person may appear as the Four of Spades in your spread, or the spread of someone else, instead of their authentic Four of Diamonds because they want to discuss work matters, are ill, or have a heavy, dark agenda to discuss with you. Learn about the emotions of each suit to interpret the "changing of the clothes" and emotions better. The suits are dynamic, just like our emotions when they appear in someone else's spread, but the card numbers and the Jacks, Queens, and Kings are static. For example, the Fours will only appear as a Four of whatever suit they feel like showing up in while we interact with them, but that doesn't mean their External card has permanently changed. It only means that's how they choose to appear on that day or how we choose them in that moment. They will never appear as another number except possibly their Primordial, Mirror, Imprint, or Shadow codes.

About fifteen years ago, I had a male friend interested in collaborating with me on a business level. He kept asking me about one specific product I was selling in hopes of bypassing me as the middleman and going directly to my vendor for the entire profit. I kept saying no for years. Giving that information away would make him my competitor, so I would have to be stupid to agree. One day, he insisted he wanted to visit me for the weekend to socialize and have fun. He even flirted with me, which made me question his true motives. Did he genuinely enjoy my company as a friend, or was he secretly planning to increase his income by convincing me to give up my contact with that vendor by seducing me over a glass of wine, or did he genuinely want some romance? Which one was it?

The only way I could discover how he truly felt about me and the real reason for his visit was to look at his card spread for that weekend to see how he perceived my External Four of Hearts. Indeed, he had me as the Four of Diamonds all weekend and not my authentic Four of Hearts. What did this tell me? He had ulterior motives for money, disguised by the diamond's suit on my 4 of Hearts. If he were genuinely interested in me as a friend or lover, he would have had the Four of Hearts, my authentic card, in his spread for that weekend visit. Consequently, I was prepared! Thanks to the 52-Star Code System, I was not blindsided, manipulated, or disappointed. People can try to fool you, but the cards don't lie if you know how to read them.

The suits are akin to clothing. They can be taken off, changed up, or flipped around when they appear in your predicatory spreads. Suits can indicate how someone may act or behave during the cycles they emerge in your spread with different clothing. For example, when a client books a session with me, how I appear in their weekly spread foreshadows how they might perceive their reading with me. For instance, if my suits and card numbers are reversed, I will be perceived as something I am not. Consequently, a session like that will go poorly. I canceled a new client once when I saw this alignment in her spread the day we were supposed to meet. She had me as the Six of Hearts and Four of Clubs on that day in her spread with her stress code. I knew she would experience massive stress during the session, and there would be undertones or blatant feelings of disconnectedness and tension, no matter how I endeavor to explain my findings.

By canceling, I saved her money and prevented the stress we might have endured during the session. I am an empath and can feel someone's stress a mile away, and I prefer to work under supportive circumstances. She had her stress card on the day she booked her session, and the landlords (tiny cards underneath the Vertical and Horizontal main cards) under her stress card were the Four of Clubs and Six of Hearts. That represented how she would perceive me. She had "me" (my cards) spun and twisted up with the numbers, and the suits reversed. Under these circumstances on that particular day, she would never truly hear what I would share with her in the way I hoped to be perceived. Some psychologists label a failed session like this as an unfortunate "selective listening" case, meaning the client would only hear what she wanted. This session was a nightmare waiting to happen, and I was glad I had the insight with the cards to know ahead. My intuition initially propelled me to check her cards before our session.

Let's look at another example of how the suits can change. When we inspect all attributes of all the Aces in the deck, the Ace of Spades is the most challenging and evolutionary Star Code. If you know anyone who is an Ace of Hearts, Diamonds, or Clubs and you plan time to have a joyous occasion or collaborate with them in business to ensure the most harmonious exchange, don't agree to meet them when they appear in YOUR spread at the Ace of Spades. You may look at your spread and think the Ace of Spades emerging in your spread is another person and has nothing to do with your Ace friend, right? Wrong. Your Ace of Diamonds, Ace of Hearts, or Ace of Club's friend may appear in the Spades suit in your spread. However, each scenario is unique, so we must consider every factor. Maybe you have two Aces you are contending with that day? Perhaps one is authentically the Natal Ace of Spades? In that case, meeting that person would be okay because they show up authentically. However, the other Aces may get lumped into that Ace of Spades portal on that day or week. In that case, it might be best to reschedule them.

For example, I had a double Ace of Diamonds best friend for many years. We had an unfortunate falling out due to someone's gossip. I miss her, especially since she is my blessed Star Code 27. We often had so much fun meeting for sushi or shopping together. I learned the hard way about rescheduling with her when I noticed I had the Ace of Spades on the day we sched-uled something together. Each time I ignored that Ace of Spades and met with her over the years, our conversations went sour despite the whispers yelling in my heart and the Ace of Spades jumping out at me. Sometimes, the appearance of her Ace of Spades in my spread made her cancel because she was sick. Spades can represent illness, among other things. Thank-fully, this happened only occasionally with her. We usually had a fun time together. It's always best to meet with people for a joyous occasion when they appear in their authentic "clothing" (suit) on that day, week, or 52-day cycle. This principle applies to all Star Codes, composites, places, things, and events with a measurable Star Code.

> Stay present. Watch how time moves through you. We don't chase time. The more we are present, the faster we attract what we desire. Be happy now.

Soul Genealogy

When the Grandmothers speak, the earth will
be healed. - Hopi Proverb

Every family shares one or two main card themes. My family's
main themes are the 4♥'s and the 4♦, with the Q♣ as a close
third theme. Between me, my two sisters, and my mother and
father, we share nine 4♥ cards and six 4♦ cards. The rest of
the cards still matter but are not the main focus of our family.
Our family incarnated together in this lifetime to learn about the
Neptunian Dirty Double Stargate of Red Fours. The theme and
lesson behind that Stargate interface with the Eight of
Diamonds. Why? When we add the star codes of that Dirty
Double, the Eight of Diamonds is the total. 4♥ Star Code 4.
4♦ Star Code 30. Math: 4 + 30 = 34. Eight Diamonds is Star
Code 34. Adding the External cards of my immediate family also
adds to Star Code 34, the Eight of Diamonds. Math: Mother
Jack of Diamonds Star Code 37. Sister Amy Four of Diamonds
Star Code 30. Sister Lisa Jack of Clubs Star Code 24. Father
King of Diamonds Star Code 39. 4 + 30 + 24 + 37 + 39 = 134.
Subtract 52 repeatedly until the total is under 52. The second
total is 82. The third total is 30, the Four of Diamonds. Even

when you add their other Cusper cards to the mix, we still get Four of Diamonds, the Primordial Four of Hearts.

Lessons around this Stargate are inescapable for our family. My family themes involve lessons concerning money, power, self-worth, marriage, divorce, financial security, home, ego, narcissism, and family love. My parents fought their entire marriage and finally divorced when I was fourteen. We are a family of entrepreneurs. My parents are unusually wealthy and powerful but never shared any money with me, and I hardly asked even though I was tempted. Our family is divided and wounded; many of us don't talk to one another. Without too much information or violating the privacy of my family, we have all noticed narcissism, ego, and power struggles in matters of the heart and the bank. Money was never shared in a fair way or at all. I dread the debacles we may face when inheritances and "wills" become a focus. Both my parents are still alive as I write, but not well. My entire family is rooted in a Stargate; it's been a wild ride! Stargates are very unstable and unpredictable!

I used the External cards for each family member to formulate most of the layers, though I did include the Internal cards. My family's chart is perhaps a little more complicated than most families because my sister Amy and my mother are Cuspers. Cuspers usually "family" together. My husband and daughter are also Cuspers, but I didn't include them in the chart below because it might have been considered overkill for this book. However, my former and current husband were born as External Fours. They fit into my birth family of many Fours. The Name card can be found on my website using a widget calculator to calculate the letters. This can also be done manually using the Star Code Letter Value Key at the back of this book. Each letter has a numerical value.

Record Your Family Layers

The chart at the end of this chapter reflects how many of each card my family shares. By recording all the cards in a family, we can discover the family theme and why they chose each other in this lifetime. Find the card that repeats most frequently among all the members. Notice my family's chart, the Four of Hearts, Four of Diamonds, and Queen of Clubs were the most common cards in our family. I listed those three cards in the first upper left row of one of the charts at the back of this chapter. I did it this way because it was the most coherent for me, but you can develop your chart in any order or format. Hopefully, you won't have too many family Cuspers because it creates extra work reading their charts and doing this assignment. However, it's an excellent challenge that can sharpen your Star Code reading skills. My mother and sister are Cuspers, and I would be remiss if I didn't include their two cards for each category.

The chart reflects how many of each card my family shares. We can discover the family theme by tracking all the cards in common. Find the card that repeats most frequently among all the members. Notice below the Four of Hearts, Four of Diamonds, and Queen of Clubs were the most common cards in our family. The Four of Hearts and Four of Diamonds create a complete Stargate in the Neptune row of the Earth Template, which causes instability and karmic challenges. This may be why our family is so troubled and divided. I listed those three cards in the first upper left row. I did it this way because it was the most coherent for me, but you can develop your chart anyway. Hopefully, you won't have too many family Cuspers because it creates extra work reading their charts and doing this assignment. However, it's an excellent challenge that can sharpen your reading skills. My mother and sister are Cuspers, and I would be remiss if I didn't include their two cards for each category.

. . .

Below are the sum totals of the cards my family has in common with each other, weaving us into a quantum entanglement within the Neptunian Red Four's Stargate. See the Sample Chart to record your family's cards on the following page.

4♥: 9	5♦: 4	2♣: 2	2♠: 2	3♣: 2	Q♥: 1
4♦: 6	2♠: 3	K♥: 2	10♠: 2	9♦: 2	K♣: 1
Q♣: 4	10♣: 3	K♦: 2	9♣: 2	7♠: 2	J♥: 1
6♣: 3	10♥: 3	8♠: 2	K♠: 2	4♠: 2	
6♠: 3	Q♦: 3	8♦: 2	5♥: 2	9♠: 1	
J♦: 3	10♦: 2	7♠: 2	4♣: 2	7♦: 1	

❝ When we discover who we are, it influences our future. - Anna Swayne (Ancestry.com)

The next page shows my family's genealogy chart, where the Four of Hearts appears nine times, and the Four of Diamonds appears six times. The following page offers a chance for my readers to create their own family genealogy card chart and discover your family's theme.

Name Private	Name Private	Name Private	Name Private	Name Private
Relation Self	Relation Sister	Relation Sister	Relation Mother	Relation Father
Birthday 11/29	Birthday 4/17	Birthday 1/29	Birthday 6/6	Birthday 5/6
Cusper (if applicable) NA	Cusper (if applicable) 4/16	Cusper (if applicable) NA	Cusper (if applicable) 6/7	Cusper (if applicable) NA
External 4♥	External 4♦ 5♦	External J♣	External J♦10♦	External K♦
Internal 6♣	Internal 6♣	Internal 4♥	Internal 4♥ 8♠	Internal 4♣
Shadow 4♠	Shadow 5♠9♦	Shadow 9♦	Shadow 3♠Q♣	Shadow 3♣
Mirror 10♠	Mirror 5♥ 3♣	Mirror 10♥	Mirror J♣ Q♠	Mirror 7♠
Imprint 10♣	Imprint 10♠ K♠ A♣ J♥	Imprint 2♦	Imprint 2♠ 5♦	Imprint 4♥
Primordial 9♠	Primordial 4♥ Q♦	Primordial Q♠	Primordial 8♣ Q♣	Primordial J♦
Blessed A♦	Blessed A♦ 6♠	Blessed K♠	Blessed K♣ 2♣	Blessed 4♠
Stress K♦	Stress 3♣ Q♣	Stress 5♦	Stress 10♦ 10♣	Stress 10♥
Decanate 6♣	Decanate 6♠7♠	Decanate 4♥	Decanate4♦A♥	Decanate 6♥
Healing-in Q♠	Healing-in J♣3♣	Healing-in 5♥	Healing-in 54♣	Healing-in 7♦
Healing-out 4♦	Healing-out 2♠7♠	Healing-out 9♦	Healing-out 4♥ 8♠	Healing-out 6♥
Stargate Partner (if applicable)4♦6♣	Stargate Partner (if applicable) 4♥ 6♣	Stargate Partner (if applicable) 4♦	Stargate Partner (if applicable) 10♥ 4♦	Stargate Partner (if applicable) K♥
First Name Karyn 4♠	First Name K♥	First Name 2♣	First Name 8♦	First Name 4♥
Higher Octave 8♦	Higher Octave K♠ 8♠	Higher Octave 2♣	Higher Octave 9♥ 10♣	Higher Octave 10♥
Exaggerated Q♥	Exaggerated Q♦	Exaggerated Q♣	Exaggerated Q♦	Exaggerated J♦

Name	Name	Name	Name	Name
Relation	Relation	Relation	Relation	Relation
Birthday	Birthday	Birthday	Birthday	Birthday
Cusper (if applicable)	Cusper (if applicable)	Cusper (if applicable)	Cusper (if applicable)	Cusper (if applicable)
External	External	External	External	External
Internal	Internal	Internal	Internal	Internal
Shadow	Shadow	Shadow	Shadow	Shadow
Mirror	Mirror	Mirror	Mirror	Mirror
Imprint	Imprint	Imprint	Imprint	Imprint
Primordial	Primordial	Primordial	Primordial	Primordial
Blessed	Blessed	Blessed	Blessed	Blessed
Stress	Stress	Stress	Stress	Stress
Decanate	Decanate	Decanate	Decanate	Decanate
Healing-in	Healing-in	Healing-in	Healing-in	Healing-in
Healing-out	Healing-out	Healing-out	Healing-out	Healing-out
Stargate Partner (if applicable)	Stargate Partner (if applicable)	Stargate Partner (if applicable)	Stargate Partner (if applicable)	Stargate Partner (if applicable)
First Name	First Name	First Name	First Name	First Name
Higher Octave	Higher Octave	Higher Octave	Higher Octave	Higher Octave
Exaggerated	Exaggerated	Exaggerated	Exaggerated	Exaggerated

The Reign of the 8 of Diamonds

This card is located at the top center of the Earth Template and is known as the Sun card. It belongs to the Red Eight Stargate, partnered with the Eight of Hearts. Its traits are akin to those of the Sun: shining, powerful, brilliant, masculine, commanding, and regal. Many CEOs, leaders, presidents, kings, parliaments, entrepreneurs, and governments embody this Star Code on some level. No doubt, the number eight seems to rule time on Earth.

What is an Analemma?

If you looked at the Sun at the same time each day, from the same place, would it appear at the exact location in the sky? If the Earth were not tilted and its orbit around the Sun were perfectly circular, then, yes, it would. However, the Earth's 23.5-degree tilt and slightly elliptical orbit combined generate this figure "8" pattern of where the Sun would appear simultaneously throughout the year. The pattern is called an analemma.

The Sun will appear at its highest point in the sky and

highest point in the analemma during summer. In the winter, the Sun is at its lowest point. The in-between times generate the rest of the analemma pattern. Analemmas on the other planets have different shapes entirely![1]

There are two kinds of solar time on Earth. 1. Apparent Solar Time tracks the diurnal motion of the Sun. 2. Mean Solar Time tracks a theoretical Sun with uniform motion along the celestial equator. Apparent Solar Time can be obtained by measuring the Sun's current position, as indicated by a sundial. A steady clock for the same place would characterize Mean Solar Time. The equation of time is the analemma's east or west component with an eight-shaped curve representing the angular offset of the Sun from its position on the celestial sphere as viewed from Earth.[2]

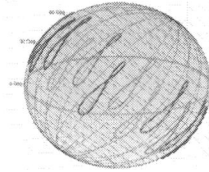

The Earth Template has been depicted as a rectangle for centuries but was initially shaped like a Diamond. In my next book, I will include the Diamond Shaped Earth Template. When we look at the Earth Template, imagine the Eight of Diamonds at the top stretched upwards, and the Eight of Hearts at the bottom stretched downwards. Imagine the Ace of Diamonds being stretched to the left and directly across from it, the Six of Diamonds being stretched to the right. It forms the shape of a Diamond when we pull it in these four directions. Notice the Ace of Diamonds, symbolizing the number 1, and the Six of Diamonds spun upside down? The Ace of Diamonds, as the number 1, is immune to the spin because it's still the shape of the number 1 no matter how you spin it. The Six of Diamonds, when spun upside down, morphs into a number 9. It would still

---

1. https://solar-center.stanford.edu/art/analemma.html
2. https://en.wikipedia.org/wiki/Equation_of_time

be immune to annihilation when spun because it forms another valid number. It also activates the 9-6 Exchange black hole portal. For example, if we spin a 2, 3, 5, or 7, they don't morph into anything we recognize.

Here's the math when we add all the Star Codes of the four cards that get "stretched" in the Earth Template to form a Diamond, as mentioned above:

8 of Diamonds = 34.
6 of Diamonds = 32.
8 of Hearts = 8.
Ace of Diamonds = 27.

The formula is 34 + 32 + 8 + 27 = 101. Subtract 52 = 49. The Star Code for the Ten of Spades is directly interchangeable with the Ace of Spades and is located directly below the Eight of Diamonds. (I have lots to say about the Ten of Spades, but I will save that for my 52 Star Code Student Guide.)

One of the 52-Star Code Rules: Cards of the same suit can be added at face value. When we add the horizontal Ace and Six of Diamonds at face value, it totals Seven of Diamonds, a wealth card contingent upon authenticity and accountability. When we are in debt, the 6 of Diamonds spins to the 9 of Diamonds. Our country and the world are in massive debt, so 6 of Diamonds has been spun and energetically upside down as I wrote this book. At face value, we can add the 9 of Diamonds and the Ace of Diamonds to equal the 10 of Diamonds, located smack dab in the middle of the Earth Template, where it forms the Jupiterian Dirty Double Red Ten Stargate. Also, four rows away in an upward direction, it interfaces with the Ten of Spades, which "Spades" the Ten of Diamonds. I use "Spades" as a verb, describing its innate action. Spades herald lessons, death, karma, old age, secrets, and endings on the dark side. It aligns with the planet Saturn.

When the 6 of Diamonds spin upside down, it affects the entire Earth Spread, causing massive debt, Stargate activations, secrets, lessons, and hardship involving money, energy, luck, and divine grace. This is akin to the story about the chicken and the egg. Which comes first? I will tell you, the global debt came first, which spun the Six of Diamonds upside down. Before the debt arrived, deception, greed, and power struggles gave rise to the debt. The only remedy is for everyone to eliminate debt, be honest, kind, and transparent, and recalibrate the monetary system. Start with yourself and visualize the entire world following suit. Dream a new world into being.

According to Vedic scripture and many other indigenous ancient cultures, we live in the Kali Yuga, a Sanskrit word meaning a time of darkness. When it ends, we enter the Sat Yuga, the age of truth on a New Earth. The Old Earth Card Template will no longer apply on that New Earth. We will have a new language of the stars, reflecting the new consciousness. The New Earth template will begin with the Seven of Diamonds, displacing the Ace of Hearts. When we quadrate the cards so that the Seven of Diamonds is in the lead, we find Queen of Spades where the Ace of Diamonds is. We find the Five of Hearts, where the Six of Diamonds is. Adding the Star Codes of those two cards equals the Four of Hearts, the card of love, family, and marriage, and the foundation for emotional wellness. That means the New Earth will prioritize these principles, much like the Garden of Eden, where we all follow the Golden Rule in unity consciousness or higher, and family comes first.

> *Raise your words, not voice. It is rain that grows flowers, not thunder."*-Rumi

Golden Rule

Surround yourself with people who make you happy. People who make you laugh, who help you when you're in need. People who genuinely care. They are the ones worth keeping in your life. Everyone else is just passing through.–
Karl Marx

I am a recovering Catholic, though I love many things about Catholicism. I have fond memories of singing beautiful songs with everyone in church. The Golden Rule is one of my all-time favorites, though. I later discovered that all religions have a similar Golden Rule, using different words. Kindness is my new religion, aligning beautifully with The Golden Rule: "Do unto others as you would like to have done unto you."

If you are intrigued by this and want to learn more, I highly recommend reading more about the Golden Rule at the link below: Iep.utm.edu/goldrule

The Golden Rule

Buddhism.
Hurt not others with that which pains yourself.

Christianity:
Do unto others as you would have them do unto you.

Hinduism:
Treat others as you would yourself be treated.

Islam:
Do unto all men as you wish to have done unto you.

Judaism:
What you yourself hate, do to no man.

Native American:
Live in harmony, for we are all related.

Sacred Earth:
Do as you will, as long as you harm no one.

Stargate Exploration

There is a way from me to you that I am
constantly searching for. - Rumi

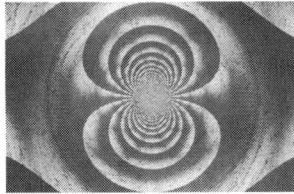

Stargates are doorways into other dimensions, densities, lokas, planes of existence, and levels of consciousness. I affectionately call the Stargates found in the Earth Template of the 52 Star Code System Dirty Doubles. It was just a silly nickname I used upon their initial discovery, and it stuck. Stargates usually appear in sets of two, like two doors, two windows, or two gates, which means they have dualistic properties in communion with the Earth's harmonics on one side of the intersection. The other side of the intersection might be entirely outside of time and space, igniting another harmonic unassociated with the duality of Earth. Stargates are associated with wormholes, black holes, and other infinite momentum tunnels existing outside of time and space as we know on Earth. They are traversable instantaneously once they become ignited and are governed by the south and north poles of the Moon, which are intersections in the cosmos we call Rahu and Ketu. Rahu will swallow us into a Stargate, while Ketu will spit us out randomly. Rahu may push the Stargate upward, while Ketu may push the Stargate downward. These intersections are also known as the Nodes of the

Moon and are responsible for eclipses. The Nodes are tricksters because they are unpredictable and enjoy remaining an elusive mystery. There are many other definitions of this term, but this definition is most pertinent for this book.

The Ruler (or landlord) of all 9 Stargates is the Five of Clubs, Star Code 18, The Eclipse Card. When we want to know more about a house or apartment, we interview the landlord, right? That's how we may begin to understand the purpose and function of these 9 Stargates. We can know they have an eclipse-like nature. Eclipses are transformational, purifying, and unpredictable. They occur by obstructing the great luminaries in the sky. They represent quantum darkness consequently. However, the dark and light live on the same street, so to speak. All dark news is light news in the end because the Universe is always conspiring to bless us in the most mysterious ways. Eclipses can cause delusion and temptation, increase the speed of time, and increase the proliferation of bacteria, viruses, and food poisoning. However, I have also witnessed good things unfold during eclipses and Stargate transits, but they are just not as common. It would be best not to plan an auspicious event, like a wedding near or on an eclipse or Stargate days in the calendar year. Also, if you have a Stargate personal transit in an unfavorable planetary cycle in your daily card spread, this would not be a favorable time to plan an event or take risks.

Do any of your layers belong to any of the nine Stargates in the Earth Template? If you have an External, Internal, Imprint, Shadow, Mirror, or Decanate card that belongs to any of the cards circled in white in the Earth Template below, ask yourself, "Have I found my Stargate partner?" Search for birthdays at the back of the book. If you don't know someone's birthday, try Mylife.com for Facebook. Please find the Dirty Double Stargates on the Earth Template circled in black in the photograph on the following page.

. . .

Please notice the Nine Stargates circled in black on the next
page. They are cards of the same color suit (red or black)
and the same number or face card. Note that the Red Eights
are not beside one another when the Earth Template is flat;
however, they form a most potent Stargate when rolled or
folded. I affectionately named them the Dirty Doubles when
I first discovered them.

The Earth Template

Mercury

Venus

Mars

Jupiter

Saturn

Uranus

Neptune

Stargate Birthdays

Are you a "Walking Stargate?" Do you belong to the Stargate Family?

AD/AH	3S/3C	4D/4H	6S/6C	7D/7H	8H/8D	9S/9C	10D/10H	KD/KH
July 14	May 29	July 11	May 26	July 8	Dec 23 (Cap)	May 23	July 5	July 2
	Aug 23		Sept 18			June 21 (Gemini)	Aug 29	Aug 26
	Sept 21 (Virgo)		Aug 20 (Virgo)			Sept 15		Sept 24 (Virgo)
Sept. 21, August 20, Dec. 23, June 21 and Sept. 24 are birthday on the cusps of their sign.								

This chart reveals famous people born on the Dirty Double Stargate days. I refer to them as "Walking Stargate People." There are other formulas for identifying "Walking Stargate People" when we apply the Decanate Ruling Cards. Learn more about that in my 52 Star Code Student Guidebook that will soon be published.

1. **AD/ AH** born on July 14th: Gerald Ford, Jane Lynch, and Conor McGregor.

2. **3S/ 3C** born on May 29th: John F. Kennedy, Bob Hope, and Annette Bening. August 23rd: Gene Kelly, Shelley Long, and Kobe Bryant. September 21st: Bill Murray, Stephen King, and Faith Hill.

3. **4D/ 4H** born on July 11th: John Quincy Adams, Lisa Rinna, and Justin Chambers.

4. **6S/ 6C** born on May 26th: Lenny Kravitz, Stevie Nicks, and John Wayne. September 18th: Lance Armstrong, Jason Sudeikis, and Jada Pinkett Smith. August 20th: Robert Plant, Amy Adams, and Connie Chung.

5. **7D/ 7H** born on July 8th: Kevin Bacon, Toby Keith, and John D. Rockefeller.

6. **9S/ 9C** born on May 23rd: Joan Collins, Mitch Albom, and Drew Carey. June 21st: Wiliam, Prince of Wales, Chris Pratt, and Juliette Lewis. September 15th: Tommy Lee Jones, Oliver Stone, and Prince Harry.

7. **10D/ 10H** born on July 5th: Huey Lewis, Edie Falco, and Marc Cohn. August 29th - Michael Jackson, Ingrid Bergman, and Charlie Parker.

8. **KD/ KH** born on July 2nd: Margot Robbie, Larry David, and Lindsay Lohan. August 26th: Macaulay Culkin, Melissa McCarthy, and Mother Teresa. September 24th: Jim Henson, F. Scott Fitzgerald, and Linda Eastman McCartney.

9. **8D/8H** born December 23rd: Alexander I of Russia, Emperor Zhenzong, Queen Silvia of Sweden, Wesley Clark, The former first lady of France, Carla Bruni-Sarkozy, and Rock singer Eddie Vedder (Pearl Jam).

I am not a scientist, nor do I claim to be an expert on Stargates, so I thank my Spirit companions and Gatekeepers of this 52-Star Code System who downloaded this information for me as I wrote. I am still collecting stories and data about how my clients and friends experience personal transit Stargates (when they occur in the direct and vertical spreads for a day) and the collective transits Stargates as listed inside the table on the following page. I have asked friends and clients who belong to certain Stargates to track and report how they unfolded for them so I could better understand and crack the codes on the function, purpose, and attributes Stargates embody. I would be delighted if you could share your Stargate stories with me! Mark the dates on your calendar and report your observations to me via email. I would be so grateful. Please include your birthday.

Rahu and Ketu, like Bonnie and Clyde, work in tandem, creating radical extreme conditions. We can find eight Stargates in the Earth Template in the photo in this chapter. I circled the Stargates in white. Do any of your layers belong to one of these Stargates? There are also birthdays when their external and internal cards create an entire Stargate. These people embody the qualities of Stargates and may struggle to remain grounded and centered in this life because they have one foot in this world and another foot in another. They may be overly sensitive, psychic, powerful, and vulnerable. Depending on their consciousness, they may also act as conduits for divine messages or dark energies.

Michael Jackson, the King of Pop music, born August 29, embodied an entire Dirty Double Stargate. He played the External Ten of Hearts and Internal Ten of Diamonds in the Jupiter row of the Earth Template. Jupiter governs money, and that particular Dirty Double Stargate has the propensity to be one of the wealthiest in the Template. It also interfaces with the other Jupitarian Stargate because the Ten of Heart's Primordial Code is the Ace of Diamonds, which belongs to the other Jupitarian Stargate. On top of that, his Vedic astrology chart shows a full bright moon in his first house, making him highly visible, sweet, and shiny. He was married to his music, according to his chart. Since he was a walking Stargate, his music may have been unintentionally channeled, downloaded, or gifted to him from other realms. His Imprint code was the Seven of Spades, one of the two presence healers in the deck. His music healed the world and brought joy to so many. His Primordial Imprint Code was the King of Spades, the God card. His Vedic astrology chart reveals the Mother Wound, and his Primordial Internal code is the Queen of Clubs, providing confluence for this finding. He had only one foot in this world, while the other was in another. Read more about the Mother Wound in the Mother Wound chapter of this book.

My gut tells me Michael only felt alive and grounded while dancing and singing. Michael may have felt lost during the other times. It was hard to be him and stay grounded, as his talent consumed him. He may have become a workaholic because he was lost when he wasn't working. Money grew from trees because he was a walking Stargate but hardly rested enough to enjoy it. On the other hand, this Stargate could have opened downward, leaving him broke. Why did it open upwards? He was born during the two hours of August 29 when the moon was on the eastern horizon in the sidereal constellation of Aquarius. Aquarius indicates revolutionary endeavors that reach the masses. The moon denotes publicity. It was a powerful, bright moon, making him very visible. Full moons in someone's chart often means disharmony or divorce between parents, which can be very unsettling for someone as sensitive as Michael. Most artists learn how to funnel their childhood pain with their art in adulthood. He was destined for fame and fortune, causing the Stargate to open upward and money and talent to shower down upon him.

If you belong to one of the Stargates in the Earth Template, it might be fun and insightful to reflect on your life or examine your current life to discover your Stargate partners and then learn about the subliminal themes. There are no Stargates in the Mercury and Uranus rows of the Earth Template, but there are two Stargates in the Jupiter and Neptune rows. There is only one Stargate in the Venus, Saturn, and Mars rows.

Since there are nine Stargates in the Earth Template, we can assume they have something to do with an ending, culmination, or rebirth. When you read the chapters of each card that creates these Stargates, you will discover the themes and lessons for each one. The Five of Clubs is the Star Code that dominates all nine Stargates in the Earth Template. After we add all the Star Codes that belong to these Stargates, we reduce the total by subtracting 52 repeatedly. The final value is Five of Clubs Star Code 18.

These Stargates interact with one another, almost like revolving doors horizontally and vertically. When an entire Stargate appears in your card spread in the vertical and direct positions, something powerful may happen on that day for you, favorable or unfavorable, depending on the planetary day it lands on. It can be akin to the 9/6 exchange. Since the Nodes of the Moon govern these Stargates, they remain unpredictable but controllable with different states of consciousness and intention. (Read more about this at the beginning of this book in the Stargate chapter.)

It's insightful and fun to find your Stargate partners. They are often born into families; they marry one another or become arch-enemies or best friends forever. They will never produce anything neutral, which is not in their nature.

My birthday belongs to two Dirty Double Stargates occupying the Neptune row in the Earth Template. My External Four of Hearts belongs to the Neptunian Dirty Double Stargate of Red

Fours, and my Internal Six of Clubs belongs to the Neptunian Dirty Double Stargate of Black Sixes. My Red Fours have the themes, lessons, and gifts belonging to the Eight of Diamonds. My Black Sixes have themes, lessons, and gifts in exchange with the Venusian Dirty Double Stargate of Black Nines, the Five of Clubs, and the Queen of Hearts, igniting the Mother Wound, self-esteem issues, goddess issues, eclipse-like experiences. Both my sisters belong to the Red Fours, as well as my lifelong best college friend. I dated several Black Six and Nine people and had my most painful lessons with them.

Below is a list of the nine Stargates, aka Dirty Doubles. If you have a Natal, Internal, Shadow, Mirror, Decanate, or Primordial card that belongs to any of these Stargates, finding your Dirty Double partner might be fun and insightful. They usually family together or find one another somehow. Most of my best friends —over my entire life— have belonged to one of the Stargates. My whole birth family each belongs to a Stargate. My 4 of Hearts External and 6 of Clubs Internal belong to separate Stargates. I immediately get along with most people with a Stargate layer of any type. Remember, the Five of Clubs is the Ruler of all the Stargates, so they are included in the Stargate family of eighteen cards. Former President Trump was indicted the year he had the full-blown Black Sixes Stargate in his Saturn cycle. I call these Dirty Doubles because that's the silly nickname I gave them upon discovery. Silly names are catchy, so it stuck. I knew they were significant, unpredictable, powerful, and transformative because the Eclipse card rules them, the Five of Clubs, Star Code 18, hence the nickname. Notice there are no Dirty Doubles in the Mercury and Uranus rows in the Earth Template. Mercury and Uranus are higher octaves of each other and have their own dirty trickster traits.

Venus: 9S/9C = 5C
Venus: 7D/7H = AS
Mars: KD/KH = KS
Jupiter: AD/AH = 2D
Jupiter: 10D/10H = 7S
Saturn: 3S/3C = 6H
Neptune: 6S/6C = QH
Neptune: 4D/4H = 8D
Crownline: 8D/8H = 3S
Total after subtracting 52 repeatedly:
5D, Star Code 18

66 *Living in a world without the hidden laws of nature is like not knowing the language of the country in which one was born.* -Hazrat Inayat Khan (Sufi musician and writer)

Stargate Case Study

She ignited the only Stargate that rules the Mother Wound when she chose May 26th as her wedding day.

I knew a mother and son who formed the Neptunian Stargate of Black Sixes. They kept losing each other on many levels for decades. See the table below where the son's Internal card is the Six of Spades, and the mother's is the Six of Clubs.

This particular Stargate is one of the most extreme because it is also part of the 9/6 Black Hole in the Earth Template inside the Neptune row. It is also the one holding the theme of the Mother Wound because when we add the Star Codes of the two black sixes that form this Stargate, subtracting 52, we get 12, the Queen of Hearts –The Earth Mother Star Code.

Neptune governs drugs, deception, delusion, insanity, disorders, romance, tides, emotions, poisons, confusions, and psychic abilities. It is a higher octave of Venus. The next most extreme Stargate is the Venusian Stargate of Black Nines. There is no Black Hole in the Venus line; however, its Nine of Spades is the Shadow card of the Six of Spades, forming a subtle Black Hole of its own in the Venus line of the Earth Template. Venus is a softer version of Neptune.

When someone finds their Stargate partner, the relationship will have karmic overtones from unresolved lifetimes. Their union will cause them to perceive everything about their relationship at a heightened state of polar extremes, favorable or unfavorable. The one formed by this mother-and-son case study was very challenging, especially for the mother, cultivating severe emotions, events, and death-like moments, oscillating between extreme sorrow and extreme joy.

Their story is a classic, extraordinary, heartbreaking Stargate tale involving a mother, son, and grandmother. The mother married the father of her son on May 26, one of the three Neptunian Black Sixes Stargate birthdays in the calendar year. This wedding ignited that Stargate, which haunted them during and after their marriage. The grandmother had Munchausen Syndrome by Proxy (MSP) and was constantly diagnosing her daughter, even though she wasn't a doctor. MSP is a relatively rare behavioral disorder. It affects a primary caretaker, often the mother. The person with MSP gains attention by seeking medical help for exaggerated or made-up symptoms of a child in their care. As healthcare providers strive to identify what's causing the child's symptoms, the deliberate actions of the parent or caretaker can often make the symptoms worse.

Interestingly, the word Munchausen adds up to Star Code 41, the Two of Spades, when we calculate each letter in that word. As I explained earlier in the book, each letter is assigned a mathematical code in the Letter Key at the back of this book. Also, all the letters in the entire term "Munchausen Syndrome by Proxy" add to a Six of Clubs, Star Code 19, part of the Double Black Six Stargate, and part of the Blue Hole Portal, as described earlier in this book. A 2 of any suit and a 6 of any suit can form a Blue Hole. However, the Two of Spades and Six of Spades union defines the classic Blue Hole.

Moreover, the daughter's Internal card is a Six of Clubs. It would be safe to say that she may have been destined to have a mother-daughter relationship that gave rise to MSP because the frequencies match up. Whenever any two (or more) people form a composite of the Two of Spades, Star Code 41, they cannot perceive each other realistically. The relationship will be clouded and carry notes of dysfunction, co-dependence, diseases, disorders, and delusions. Knowing this, we can't blame one person because composites involve two or more people. Instead, we can point to the composite and work from there, using understanding and wisdom, recognizing the karmic soul contract, and acknowledging the lessons. Each person in the composite is accountable. (Notice that when I put the word Munchausen in the Star Code Letter Calculator below, the letters add 41, which is the Star Code for Two of Spades.)

First Person

First Name	Middle Name	Last Name
Munchausen		
41	0	
Suit 1:	Two of Spades	

Second Person

First Name	Middle Name	Last Name
0	0	
Suit 2:	undefined	
Composite Suit:	Two of Spades	2♠

When the daughter gave birth to her only child, the grand-mother legally "kidnapped" her baby from the parents in plain sight. The grandmother was a wealthy, self-righteous religious zealot with an entire bible study group supporting the kidnapping. She believed she was doing the right thing, fueled by the church and her MSP syndrome. She told the court system some exaggerations and untruths about her daughter, painting her out to be mentally ill when, in fact, she was not mentally ill at all. The grandmother, whom I will refer to as the "Zealot" for the remainder of the story, and mother formed a composite of Star Code 41 together when adding her daughter's External Star Codes: 4 + 37 = 41, the Two of Spades. (Read about how to calculate composites at the beginning of the book.)

Notice the Two of Spades is the Shadow card to the Neptunian Stargate of the Six of Spades, and it's part of the dysfunctional Blue Hole Portal. (Find that chapter in the table of contents for more info.) When anyone makes a Blue Hole composite with another person, especially a Two of Spades, that relationship has the potential to become delusional, toxic, deranged, and dysfunctional. Each of the parties may perceive the other as crazy when, in fact, neither of them are. Everything is perception, and composites make all the difference. If someone tracked the birthdays of Munchausen Syndrome by

Proxy (MSP) cases, we would find the Two of Spades composite between the mother (or caretaker) and child at the root of the dysfunctional relationship.

The year before all this happened, the daughter stopped attending church and bible study and wanted to expand her horizons beyond Catholicism. While exploring the horizons, she discovered that God was in every person, tree, flower, ocean, and rock and was not restricted to a church. She embraced yoga and chanted "Aum" and other yogic chants that the Zealot misinterpreted as a satanic cult activity. The Zealot felt her daughter was unfit and possessed by demons because she was no longer a practicing Catholic. The Zealot became determined to rescue her grandson from the "grips of satan" and the alleged bipolar mother with all her money and power. In the court systems these days, money supercedes justice. The mother, a college graduate and honor-roll student, didn't have as much money as the Zealot and was smoked out financially, unable to afford to defend herself after the first year in court. Her son, age six, started calling the Zealot "Mom" and was completely confused about living with his grandparents instead of his real parents. However, his new home was a lovely "jail" decorated with ice cream, opulence, toys, chocolate, glitter, and anything he wanted.

The daughter wasn't allowed to visit her son unless she paid $200 per hour to a Guardian at Litem for supervision because a "parent is guilty until proven innocent" in their state. Though no mother is perfect, her family considered her a black sheep. The mother was innocent, brilliant, loving, attentive, and healthy on all levels but didn't have enough money to regain her son. No professional or any of her close friends thought she was bipolar. It was one of the many MSP fake diagnoses the zealot-grandmother grasped and was convinced of. The mother and her husband divorced the year before their son was stolen, but the father (her ex) persevered in the court system to win their son back. He was a hidden powerhouse born on a Four of Clubs day with double eight internal cards. Six years later, fifty thousand dollars poorer, he won their son back when he was twelve.

> *İnstead of clearing her own heart, the zealot tries to clear the world.* - Joseph Campbell

The Zealot inadvertently brainwashed her grandson into believing his parents were mentally ill—because that was the Zealot's unprecedented belief- and that his kidnapping was a "rescue." The grandson was returned to his mother when he was a teenager but was out of control from his grandparents' insidious psychological abuse by age thirteen, became a drug addict, and dropped out of school. In his late teens, he dated nefarious gang members and disappeared often, causing his parents to nearly lose their minds.

Throughout the rest of their lives together, the son disrespected his mother horribly and moved back and forth between his "crazy" parents, who were the most sane, healthy, innocent, and kind people I knew. The mother had always hoped her son would grow up, have a great awakening, and realize the true story instead of believing a twisted tale about being rescued by his "savior" grandparents.

Unfortunately, brainwashing can't always be undone. The son is now a highly successful entrepreneur and a recovered addict, though still struggling with his emotional body, a borderline personality disorder, and still disrespecting his mother. However, he holds his father in high esteem because his grandparents didn't brainwash him against his father as much. The hardest thing for the mother to ascertain was that not only was her son legally stolen in plain sight at the tender, impressionable age of six, but he was also emotionally stolen, even in adulthood.

Despite this broken Stargate relationship, the mother and son tried hard to mend things between them. Still, every few years, around an eclipse, they would have a massive blowout and stop talking for months, sometimes up to a year. Their severed family has deep genetic Mother Wounds. The mother oscillates in and out of hopelessness and deep grief from being misunderstood, disrespected, and losing her only child on all levels. The son doesn't grieve as much because he's comfortable in his delusion and has his grandmother to fall back on for support and further brainwashing against his mother when they have their falling outs. This volatile "on again, off again" relationship reflects a classic Stargate connection.

Interestingly, the grandfather shares the same External card as his grandson, and the Zealot's Internal card belongs to the other Neptunian Stargate of Red Fours. It is also the same Internal card as her daughter's External card (Four of Hearts). The Zealot's Decanate Ruling Card is the Four of Diamonds, igniting that Neptunian Stargate of Red Fours perpetually within herself and the whole family because most members had a Four of Hearts layer. It was their family card theme.

All Stargates become highly activated during eclipses. Stargates are partly located on Earth and in other dimensions outside time and space. This makes predicting and understanding them nearly impossible. My best advice is to stay clear of your Stargate partner, with love, during eclipses. When you unite or think of each other at any other time, the Stargates ignite, but won't be as traumatic as during the two-week eclipse windows that happen approximately twice per year, bookmarked by a solar and lunar eclipse on either end. See the table with their cards below.

Mother
External Card: 4H
Internal Card: 6C

Son
External Card: KC
Internal Card: 6S

Grandmother
External Card: JD
Internal Card: 4H

The May 26 wedding day ignited the Stargate, which gave birth to all the drama that unfolded in the family.

AD/AH	3S/3C	4D/4H	6S/6C	7D/7H	8H/8D	9S/9C	10D/10H	KD/KH
July 14	May 29	July 11	May 26	July 8	Dec 23 (Cap)	May 23	July 5	July 2
	Aug 23		Sept 18			June 21 (Gemini)	Aug 29	Aug 26
	Sept 21 (Virgo)		Aug 20 (Virgo)			Sept 15		Sept 24 (Virgo)
Sept. 21, August 20, Dec. 23, June 21 and Sept. 24 are birthday on the cusps of their sign.								

May 26 was Memorial Day weekend that year, so it seemed like a safe celebratory date, but if the mother had known what it would yield, she might have chosen a different day and be telling a different story today. May 26 is the most intense Mother Wound Stargate day of every year.

The term 'Muhurta' is a Sanskrit word meaning 'moment.' It is also a Vedic astrology term referring to a specific time frame considered astrologically auspicious for undertaking significant activities, from weddings, surgeries, natal conception, birth, and housewarming, starting a business, or initiating a major project or journey. Choosing the right Muhurta aligns intentions and actions with the divine cosmic flow, enhancing the chances of success and minimizing potential obstacles. Hire a professional to do a Muhurta before choosing a significant or critical event date. Book an appointment with me if you need one. I never recommend choosing a Stargate day as a good Muhurta for anything. They are unpredictable, extreme, and not worth the risk, even though many famous people were born on such days. There are lucky pockets of time within these Stargate days, but they are difficult to determine. We just don't know about the other less fortunate Stargate people and their stories.

66   Timing is everything, giving rise to the power of the math surrounding our birthdays.

The Mother Wound

The more a daughter knows the details of her mother's life, the stronger the daughter. - Anita Diamant

The Earth Template reflects the current time we are living on planet Earth. Sanskrit scholars call this time the Kali Yuga. The Kali Yuga is a term meaning Dark Ages. Kali is the dark Hindu goddess depicted as a frightening deity at first. Still, she truly represents the power women need during this time on Earth to defend themselves and rise above oppression from the male gender. Kali symbolizes the transformational movement from a patriarchal society into a matriarchal one. She is a force to be reckoned with and will fiercely defend victims at all costs, especially women. The Earth Template tells a story about the Kali Yuga if you know how to read the hidden, symbolic language. (Find the Earth Template at the back of this book.) We can see all the archetypes rehearsing their roles as actors, actresses, victims, villains, kings, and queens. Using our imaginations, if we superimpose the figure of the famous Davinci man over the Earth Template, we will notice his right foot crushes the Queen of Hearts while his left foot crushes the Four of Hearts. This is not to blame Mr. Davinci; I am grateful for his sacred geometry and shape because they are ideal for this metaphor. The Queen and Four of Hearts denote family, women, marriage, mothers, and the sacred feminine principle.

This vision is a metaphor for how this patriarchal rise of society during the Kali Yuga disrespects the goddess and divine mother. The Queen of Hearts represents the Earth Mother, which gives rise to the Divine Mother. The Four of Hearts portrays the sacred concepts of family, marriage, and metaphysical healing, among other things. We have been living in a time where women and children have been sex trafficked, raped, abducted, and abused on every level, where one in every two marriages end in divorce. Our new technological culture has destroyed family values while no one breaks bread together anymore; children are brainwashed by TV and social media as families become estranged, shattered, and divided.

Western astrology uses the Sun, a male-gendered star, to dictate someone's sign. Before this, we had a matriarchal rise in society, where we used Lunar astrology to worship the goddess and dictate someone's astrological sign. The Moon is the cosmic mother, while the Sun is the heavenly father. It has touted that the Moon merely reflects the Sun, diminishing her sovereignty altogether. I have read many inspiring articles and books refuting this principle, but they are not mainstream– yet. The Earth is on the cusp of a massive transformation, leaving the Kali Yuga behind while stepping into the Sat Yuga, the age of truth. However, before we can fully step in, the Earth must undergo purification, which is painful but needed before we can fully embrace the Sat Yuga. The details of how this purification looks and the timeline are still unknown to me, but we know it is upon us as I write this book.

For further confluence, using the Earth Template, we can find the Earth Mother, the Queen of Hearts, hidden behind the Neptunian Dirty Double Black Sixes Stargate. Sixes represent a backward directional flow. They take us back to remember the past and pay the emotional debt. This Stargate is in cahoots with the Venusian Dirty Double Black Nines Stargate. It is the upside-down version of the Neptunian Stargate, hiding the Queen of Hearts. The Venusian Dirty Double Black Nines Stargate completes the story with a hidden Five of Clubs, the Eclipse card: Star Code 18. It is safe to say the Earth Mother has been "eclipsed" during the Kali Yuga. The Pluto card to that Black Six Stargate is the Queen of Clubs, the Divine Mother. Though she may not be hidden behind a Stargate, she has come to transform and heal that Stargate because she is the Higher Octave of the Six of Clubs, the messenger of light. The Nine of Clubs, part of the Venusian Dirty Double Black Nines Stargate, also has a Shadow card of the Queen of Hearts, the Earth Mother. Everything is interconnected once you learn how to connect the dots.

These abovementioned Stargates both occupy the Uranus and Saturn rows in the Earth Template. Uranus governs matters of the Earth, while Saturn teaches us lessons through adversities and holds us to the letter of the law. I have found many Mother Wounds in the Vedic astrology charts of my clients, including my own. There are several ways to distinguish the Mother Wound in an astrology chart. Some distinctions are when Saturn conjoins the Moon inside one house, when Saturn aspects the Moon, or when the Moon is in its sign of debilitation, Scorpio, among other alignments.

The other way to see this affliction in the 52 Star Code System is with the Nine and Six of Clubs, where the Shadow cards are the Queen of Hearts. Several other ways to track the Mother Wound in the 52 Star Code System exist. Below are some cards that inherit the Mother Wound. Remember, the

Mother Wound extends to the Goddess Wound, giving rise to sexual afflictions. You may have had an excellent mother but suffered sexual adversities instead. The cards listed below express in any of the following primary layers: External, Internal, Decanate, Shadow, Primordial or Imprint.

Mother-Goddess-Wound Cards

Queen of Clubs, Jack of Clubs, Five of Clubs, King of Spades, Six of Diamonds, Four of Hearts, Eight of Diamonds, Ten of Clubs, Four of Diamonds, Queen of Spades, Six of Clubs, Nine of Clubs, Six of Spades, Three of Clubs, Nine of Spades, Ace of Diamonds, King of Clubs, Queen of Hearts or Ten of Diamonds. Also, any female born as a Jack or King of the Hearts, Clubs, or Spade suit may have inherited the Mother Goddess Wound.

Those who have these afflictions carry the Imprint of the collective Mother Wound in their charts, which may go back at least twelve generations. How can we heal this? When we do so, with all our heart, we heal 12 generations prior simultaneously, releasing the Imprint and liberating all women involved. Sometimes, the Mother Wound will play out as adversities between mothers and their children. This wound may not always indicate you had trouble with your mother, however. It may point to struggles, hardships, and painful situations concerning sex, possibly rape, sexual rejection, celibacy, violence or injury, or diseases of the sexual organs. To heal this wound collectively, we must start with ourselves, our mothers, and our children. The first step is always awareness. Once you know that you are carrying the Mother Wound in your 52-Star Code or Vedic astrology chart, and probably in your family tree, begin by practicing one of the Forgiveness Novenas found at the back of this book.

Understanding and forgiveness is always the key. First,

forgive yourself wholeheartedly, then forgive your mother, her mother, and the twelve generations behind you. However, forgiveness doesn't mean you must start being their best friend. You can forgive from a safe distance if need be. What matters is what is in your heart and how you feel. Perhaps she was abusive to you? You can still forgive her, knowing that she was probably abused by her mother and so on. It must start somewhere. Forgiveness doesn't make her actions or abuse right. It's not about right or wrong. It's about understanding, forgiving, and letting go lovingly. Change your story; change your life. Easier said than done! Your life will radically transform for the better once you recognize this and take the higher road. If you procrastinate with this inner work or find it too painful, master the science of meditation, breathwork, and prayer. That might be a better place to start, then proceed to the forgiveness novenas when it feels right.

Then, start respecting yourself as a woman. Know your power. Know your weaknesses. Kindness is power. If you are a man, start respecting all the women in your life. Be more loving to them, more compassionate, and above all, know you are not alone in this. Offer selfless service to homeless women, help find missing women, help heal abused women Pro Bono monthly, and pray daily for the liberation of all women. This universal affliction needs healing before we can collectively graduate into the Sat Yuga. We can also appease the Moon as the Divine Mother with this mantra: Aum Shree Chandraya Namaha. Start on a Monday, a Moon day, and repeat this mantra 108X times once daily for forty days. For proper annunciation, look it up on the internet.

I have so much more to say about this, but I will leave it at that –for now– concerning the Earth Template and the Mother-Wound. I will extrapolate more about the Father Wound and Mother Wound in my following books.

Mother Wound Symptoms

- History of being the caretaker in toxic relationships.
- Struggles with your identity and sense of self.
- Fear of intimacy and vulnerability due to lack of trust.
- Healthy boundaries seem to elude you.
- You do most things in hopes of your mother's approval.
- You criticize yourself incessantly.
- Engaging in "savior" behaviors, healing, and fixing others.
- Shame or fear lodged in your throat, unable to speak your truth.
- Tendencies to "mother" your spouse.
- Abandonment and separation anxiety dictate your emotional decisions.
- Codependence may plague you.
- Oversharing sexual trauma and concerns.
- Secretly harboring resentment toward your child.

The Loving Goddess's Before

It is not just your mother who may walk with you in spirit; it is her mother, too. And her mother's mother. And her mother's friends, who loved you by choice and not by blood. And the women before them. Generations and generations of female energy, watching in admiration as you forge ahead, living better, feeling better, accepting better than they ever did. When you feel sad, lonely, or unloved, remember them by closing your eyes and feeling them beside you. They are always with you. They burn brightly with their boundless light in everything you do. You are the 'moment in time' of many women gone before. You will lay pathways, like they did, for the unborn who plan to join you as you become a grandmother and great-grandmother and so forth. What a beautiful, unending legacy. — author unknown

Close your eyes, and consciously and with the breath, draw the Moon's light down into the third eye. Sit for a while with your eyes shut, focusing your inner awareness into the third eye area, where you can envision the orb of the Moon.

Focus the power that is granted to you into whatever you wish to see nourishing your heart, soul, and body, and manifesting in your life and in the world— perhaps more love, more contentment, more peace, or more abundance. You can finish this practice by praying for the world and honoring the Divine Mother who is also symbolized by the Moon. Take her beauty into your mind as well as your heart and give thanks for the never-ending bounty of Her love.

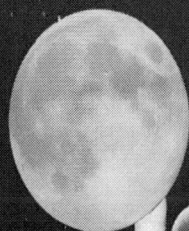

Genders and the Suits

"What is straight? A line can be straight, or a street, but the human heart, oh, no, it's curved like a road through mountains." Tennessee Williams

The Reversed Gender Card People

These people form a separate and unique tribe. They have many things in common and would do well understanding this and chumming around with other Reversed Gender card people to make their lives easier. I want to acknowledge how difficult it is to be a female King or Jack, as well as how difficult it is to be a male Queen. This situation causes many identity crises, heartache, confusion, gender fluidity, and sometimes androgyny. I have known many 'female-king-card-people' who are elderly with sad stories of how they had such a hard time in the romance department. They often stay single much longer than they want, unaware that their power unintentionally pushed away many men. Also, they may repel many men intentionally because they are bored by them if they are not as powerful. It's painful for an influential female-king-card person to dumb herself down to fit into a relationship where she is always in the driver's seat and intellectually and emotionally bored silly by her "non-royal" lover.

Be gentle with yourself and have compassion for your situation, knowing you have the skill set to rise above it, but not without adversities. However, these adversities can be softened or entirely neutralized if some of their other layers match their gender; for example, a male Queen with an Imprint or Internal card of a King or Jack may neutralize the gender issues.

Men who play External Queen cards have some of the most painful and challenging lives, especially if they have the following Internal cards: Ace, Three, Five, Seven or Nine. The good news is a Jack or King of any suit in their Imprint layer can soften the abovementioned alignment. It may not neutralize it entirely, but it will make their life easier.

I have been fascinated with the astrology and the psychology of serial killers ever since I took a class in criminal behavior. My fascination turned into a passion once I remembered a past life memory of being murdered by a serial killer and becoming very acquainted with him in Spirit during this lifetime. He is no longer stuck in the astral planes because my Shaman friends and I helped him find "the light." Later, he returned for forgiveness, and I did the Ho'oponopono Novena with him. He was born as an External Queen of Clubs and Internal Five of Clubs. Unfortunately, he did not have a Jack or King Imprint card to soften the hardships he faced during his lifetime in the 1800s. Since he had the Five of Clubs as the Eclipse card and his internal card, he could easily stay hidden from the police, out of sight. Why could he so easily hide? The great luminaries of the sky get swallowed up during an eclipse, causing quantum darkness to cover the earth. It's when the cosmic mother and father of the galaxy take their coffee break. What happens to the children when Mom and Dad are gone? Trouble! He was able to hide in the dark. Also, the Venus card that belongs to the Five of Clubs is the death card: Ace of

Spades. Venus represents women, so he had a natural bias to kill lovers secretly.

We can't make a blanket statement that all Five of Clubs card people are trouble or cause trouble, but if they also have other afflictions, we might call co-morbidities; this spells danger. Since he was a male Queen, which is a struggle in and of itself, we add the eclipse card to the mix along with some challenging upbringing and genetics; we have ourselves a potential serial killer. To understand what makes a serial killer tick and how their harmonics interface with this 52-Star Code System, I have researched innumerable serial killers' birthdays since 2018. It started as a whim that evolved into a hobby, which took a backseat once I realized at least 80 percent of them were male Queens. I no longer needed proof of my convictions, but curiosity may always propel me into further research. Many of them were and are misogynists, jealous of women, and confused about their gender. I have a secret desire to work for the FBI, helping to solve murder mysteries and protect women from these men. I could make the job of finding mysterious serial killers very easy for the police, especially killers who committed sexual murders.

- Women of the Heart's Suit Exaggerated Self: Queen of Hearts.
- Women of the Club's Suit Exaggerated Self: Queen of Clubs.
- Women of the Diamond's Suit Exaggerated Self: Queen of Diamonds.
- Women of the Spade's Suit Exaggerated Self: Queen of Spades.

Note: Women whose External card is a King can express themselves as the Queen of their suit. This would only be considered partly Exaggerated. It is partly authentic since she is simultaneously a female and a King.

- Men of the Heart's Suit Exaggerated Self: Jack of Hearts or King of Hearts.
- Men of the Clubs Suit Exaggerated Self: Jack of Clubs or King of Clubs.
- Men of the Diamond's Suit Exaggerated Self: Jack of Diamonds or King of Diamonds.
- Men of the Spade's Suit Exaggerated Self: Jack of Spades or King of Spades.

NOTE: Men whose External card is a Queen can express themselves as the King of their suit, but this would only be considered partly Exaggerated because he is simultaneously a male and a Queen. It's very hard for male Queens to discover their authenticity, but not impossible. This may also apply to the Internal card, but I have seen it stronger in the External cards.

“ Male queens have the most complex life path because our culture doesn't understand gender fluidity. They may feel misunderstood, lost, and secretly hate themselves. They are masterminds and resent rules and authority because they are above the mundane. If they are not given the proper love and support, some of them might become misogynistic serial killers and rapists. If raised by loving, non-judgemental parents, they can rule the world with love. - Karyn Chabot Martino

The Trine of Deception

"One who decieves will always find those who allow themselves to be decieved." -Niccolo Machiavelli

Three face cards are portrayed by their side profile and depicted with only one eye. When people look at you with only one eye, speak from only one side of their mouth, or have a twisted grin where only one side of their mouth smiles, beware. These three cards are the Jack of Spades, Jack of Hearts, and King of Diamonds. They sit together to form a triangle shape in the Earth Template, smack dab center. These cards have an affinity for deception, but not all people born into this trine will be deceptive. Some are born to police the Trine of Deception, but to police it easily, they must be born into it. While others are blatantly sinister, we can only use this information cautiously and not accuse anyone of deception unless proven guilty. The cards inside the middle part of the triangle are also involved somehow and suspect, but again, it will be up to you to use your discernment before jumping to conclusions.

Let's delve into some real-life examples of the Trine of Deception. Bill Gates, the renowned entrepreneur, has two Internal cards (Jack of Hearts, King of Diamonds) that belong to this trine, born on October 28. Osama Bin Laden, the infamous terrorist, was born on March 10 as the King of Diamonds. Nikolas Cruz, one of the deadliest school shooters in US history, was born September 24 as the King of Hearts and King of Diamonds. The Jack of Hearts is the Primordial King of Hearts. Frank Lucas, one of the biggest drug lords in NYC, was born on September 9 as the Two of Diamonds, Jack of Spades. Phillip Carl Jablonski, the American serial killer, was born on January 3 as a Jack of Spades. These are just a few intriguing examples highlighting the potential traits associated with the Trine of Deception.

Favorable and Unfavorable Planetary Cycles

"Beyond all ideas of good and bad, right or wrong, there is a field. I'll meet you there." - Rumi

What do I mean when I refer to cards as occupying a favorable or unfavorable planetary cycle throughout this book? Like human beings, each card has a dualistic nature. Vedic astrology refers to such planetary categories as natural functional malefics and benefics. These categories have their roots in ancient Vedic mythology, where the cosmos was in planetary war and still is. The opposing forces were named the Asuras and the Devas, unfavorable and favorable, respectively.

There is an off-shoot of Vedic Astrology called System's Approach, where they personalize and break down the favorable and unfavorable planets according to what constellation was on the Eastern horizon when you were born. For example, according to System's Approach, Mercury is unfavorable for me because Sidereal Aries was on the horizon when I was born. However, Mercury is considered neutral to the general public. Combining the System's Approach and Classic Vedic Astrology with the 52-Star Code System takes the accuracy up a notch. Still, it is impossible to share that information in this book because each of us is born at a different time of day or night and location. This would require a personal Vedic Astrology reading with me or another qualified astrologer. Watch for more information about this in my 52 Star Code Student Guide once it's published.

Favorable Planets are the Devas: Venus, Jupiter, and Moon.

Unfavorable Planets are the Asuras: Saturn, Mars, Sun, Pluto (outer planets are not involved in the war)

Chameleon or Neuter Planets: Mercury, Uranus (outer planets are not involved in the cosmic war)

Neptune: This outer planet is not involved in the cosmic war and can play out both favorably and unfavorably. Its interpretation will be contingent upon the card that occupies it.

Each card has a dark and light possibility. There is no bad card or a good card. Each card embodies both good and bad characteristics. Cards are like the keys on a piano. There are no keys on the piano that are considered bad or good. They each have different sounds. Which note resonates with you the most? Everyone will have a distinct preference. Some like the higher-pitched keys, some like the black keys, some like the white keys, and some like chords. We are made up of chords of harmonics once you begin to understand all your layers, which start with your External card. Through sacred awareness, personal growth, and accountability, we can mathematically rise a full octave in our life path and experience life from higher perspectives. As a result, we get a new card chart from which we can make predictions! The 52-Star Code System allows for and encourages spiritual growth, so we are never locked into one card for our entire lives. When we raise our frequency, we evolve eight cards away from our External card on the Earth Template, akin to an octave on the piano.

Upon understanding what I wrote above, this is where free will comes into play. We can't change the wind, but we can adjust the sails. Once we understand the 52-Star Code language, we can understand how the duality may play out and even have a hand in that unfolding. The story gets juicier once we know the planetary meanings and integrate that wisdom into each card in our spread. Yes, the more knowledge you have in astrology, the better you will be at reading the cards and knowing if they will play out favorably or unfavorably.

Many indigenous peoples say that the serpent created the earth. Other teachings tell us that this medicine (snake) was the beginning of the downfall of humanity. Knowing that those in spirit speak in symbolism, where does God fit into all this? Perhaps God is the Infinite Field of All Possibilities, Creator, Source, All That Is, Love, Sound, Truth, and Light? I will leave that for the Reader to decide.

The serpent represents our shadow-self, the unfavorable sides of the cards. The serpent has always been dead set out to destroy us, as indicated by Pluto. Not because Pluto dislikes us but because Pluto is you. We must die to be reborn. We embody both the Serpent and the Light. Is the Light trying to illuminate the buried pain only the Serpent can reveal? And have they both been working together for your highest good? We can't know evil until we know goodness and vice versa. We can't recognize white until we meet black. Once we realize the light and the dark dance together and we don't have to pick a side, we can find peace in neutrality as we weave the principles of duality together to create what might look like the Chinese yin and yang symbol, which also looks like the 9/6 portal of fish chasing one another, spiraling to create a vortex.

At the beginning of time, the Council for Planet Earth volunteered to experiment with duality and free will. Rules around "permissions" and "interference" were implemented to protect our free will. Souls daring to incarnate on Earth would go through the Veil of Amnesia, forget that they were divine beings, and step into the unknown so that we may discover that we are love over and over again. We are fearless discoverers, adventurers, pioneers, and warriors of both light and dark.

Another agreement of the free-will experiment was that every thought and action would be recorded in the Akashic records. If the balance sheet of a lifetime was in debt, the soul agreed to incarnate again to try to balance their karmic account. Earth fell behind in this third-dimensional experiment, as described above. Why? Our solar plexus chakra sends out feelers to watch for danger, and through this psychic center, we also absorb the fears of others. Because Earth is the cosmic solar plexus chakra, as represented by the Eight of Diamonds in the crown line in the Earth Template, our planet absorbs the fears of the entire universe. We have had to transmute these, making it extra hard to live on Earth. Women do most of the transmutation due to our genetic wiring, so we must heal the Cosmic Mother Wound. Once we graduate from Earth, the rest of the cosmos reveres us as winning a Purple Heart for our courage! Being human ain't easy, especially if both your External and Internal cards belong to the Neptunian row in the Earth Template, which I fondly call the Via Combusta (Path of Fire).

. . .

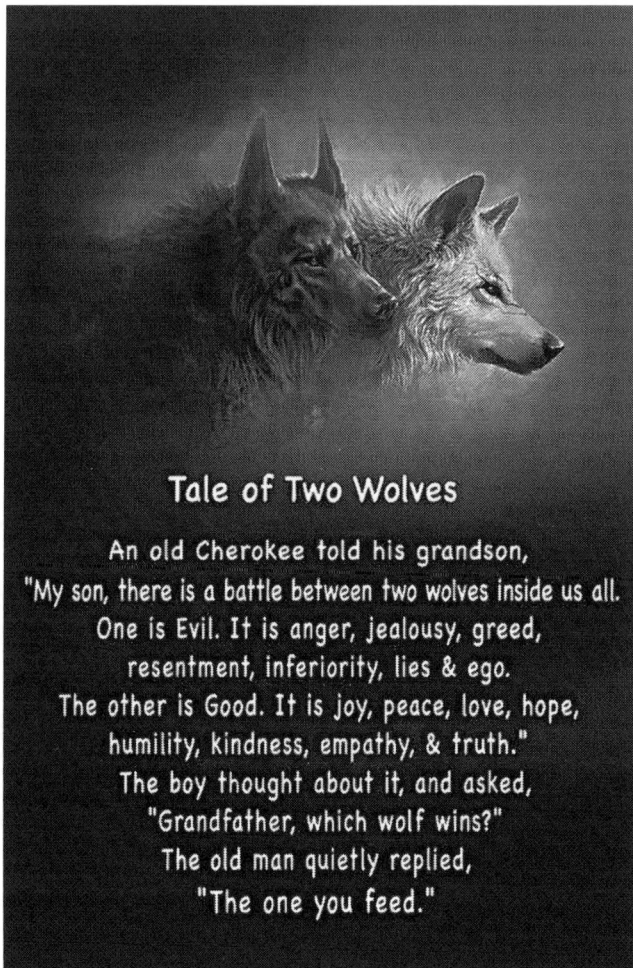

Tale of Two Wolves

An old Cherokee told his grandson,
"My son, there is a battle between two wolves inside us all.
One is Evil. It is anger, jealousy, greed,
resentment, inferiority, lies & ego.
The other is Good. It is joy, peace, love, hope,
humility, kindness, empathy, & truth."
The boy thought about it, and asked,
"Grandfather, which wolf wins?"
The old man quietly replied,
"The one you feed."

Hallowed Be Thy Name: Letter Values

Hate has four letters, but so does Love.
Enemies have seven letters, but so does
Friends. Lying has five letters, but so does
Truth. Cry has three letters, but so does Joy.
Negativity has ten letters, but so does
Positivity.

Words carry a harmonic energy, giving our language power and potential to heal or hurt. Hence, the biblical phrase, "Only say the Word, and I shall be healed." Many cultures and religions agree that letters can be assigned numerical values, especially in the Hebrew and Kabbalistic traditions. There are many ways to measure our words. Please check the back of this book to find the Star Code Letter Key.

Each letter in the word "God" equals 52, the Star Code of the King of Spades.

$$G = 33$$
$$o = 15$$
$$d = 4$$
$$Total = 52.$$

Here's another way to measure the letters in the word God:

$$God = 7 + 15 + 4 = 26.$$

G is the 7th letter, O is the 15th, and D is the 4th letter in the alphabet.

Why are there 26 letters in the English alphabet? There are many varying answers, but the human body doesn't lie. Every human has 206 bones, and we are one of the rare species that stands upright, with each of our feet and ankles containing 26 bones. The spine has 33 vertebrae. Adults have 26 vertebrae because bones fuse as we age. Every somatic cell in the body contains 26 unpaired chromosomes. There are a total of 26 elements present in the human body.

The Moon doesn't lie either. Lunation is a word derived from the root luna, meaning Moon. Earth has 13 lunations annually.

$$13 + 13 = 26$$
$$26 + 26 = 52$$
King of Hearts is Star Code 13.
King of Clubs is Star Code 26.
King of Spades is Star Code 52.

Each of the 12 ages of the zodiac is 2,160 years in length. When you multiply 2,160 by 12, for the 12 signs of the zodiac, or the 12 ages, you arrive at 25,920 years, nearly 26,000 years.

The names people call us are like music to our bodies and create a harmonic, geometrical, unique grid around us. Some music is abrasive, and some is soothing---and that matters. Unfortunately, the measured letter value of my first name, Karyn, comes to Star Code 43, which is my Shadow Code Four of Spades. I have thought about changing it, but it may not be worth it at my age because that geometrical grid has already formed a particular shape around me that may take years to reshape with a new name. If I had known this when I was younger, I would have 100 percent changed my first name. You can measure the letters in your name using the Star and Letter Code Key at the back of the book. Always subtract 52 if your total goes over 52. Or, visit my website to use the Star Code calculators.

When people call our names, they usually look at us, wanting our attention. The Sanskrit term 'drishti' pertains to gazing, referring to our eyes as windows of perception through which we mindfully experience the world around us. When we combine the power of drishti with the power of sound, which has morphed into unique energy grids from all the times people have called our names, we can almost imagine the invisible yantras and mandalas surrounding each of us. Yantra is a Sanskrit term for how mantras morph and take the shape of beautiful sacred geometrical shapes using a tonoscope, a tool for measuring sound vibrations. The science of cymatics explains this in more detail if you care to explore this subject more deeply. The term drishti also refers to the planetary aspects of our astrology charts. Planets are like people. Their gaze at you and other planets inside our astrological houses has a significant impact.

This is why words and names are so important and why when some people meet a guru, the guru might want to change their name, which would reset their outer energetic grid for the better. If our names dictate the shape of the harmonic grid around us, imagine what other words might do to us. What we say has weight and power. Being conscious means being aware of how we use words.

The more conscious we become, the more we deepen our relationship with our chosen words. Eventually, we feel what we are saying. We begin to recognize that words are not abstract, disconnected harmonics used only to convey facts but powerful transmitters of feeling and vibration. This information explains why choosing lyrics you want to listen to and music that makes you smile is important. It is essential for health. Practice witnessing how the different communication styles of the people in your life make you feel. Notice how your words come out and how others perceive them.

> ❝ *God SPOKE the world into existence over six days before resting on the seventh day, making it holy.* - Book of Genesis

You may observe that when we rush through an explanation without thinking, our words don't carry the same power as when we speak slowly with gentle conviction, allowing your listeners the time and space to process. When we compassionately listen to others before speaking, our words have more integrity. When someone feels heard, it is the first step toward healing. When we ground ourselves before speaking, we genuinely harness speech's power. Only then can our words be coherent avenues for healing and light, transmitting meaningful and joyful feelings to those we speak with.

Each alphabet letter has a harmonic, measured mathematically using the "52 Star Codes System". Using this system, you can find your Name-Star-Code because it is a mathematical composite of all the letters in a name, place, or thing. Your first name card, for example, mine is Karyn, and it is part of how the world may perceive you in a public way. This may not reflect the actual or inner you, however. It is the more public side of yourself, which may sometimes carry pretenses or masks. Our middle name denotes the most intimate part of you, often symbolizing your sexual nature. Your last name carries the sins of your forefathers, your lineage, and what your genealogy might represent. We can also measure a place, like a street name, town, state, country, or the name of a place or title of a company, for example. I extrapolate this in my 52 Star Code Student Guide.

I can determine when clients will leave their jobs by tracking the letters in their company's name. Then, I'd track that card in their spread and search for another card nearby, signifying an ending like a 9 of any suit, an Ace of Spades, or the Shadow version of the company's card, just to name a few instances of how this can be tracked.

When measuring an address using the Star Code Letter System, remember to include both the abbreviation and the complete spelling of Street or Avenue, for example. That will give you two or more cards to track, signifying that address. I have found both the abbreviated and full versions to be accurate. It depends. For example, most addresses will have two accurate frequencies because the abbreviation of Street is St, as shown on the Street sign but written out entirely at City Hall. The same goes for Avenue versus Ave, as another example. Track both because they are both accurate. Use capitals when indicated, too. Visit my website to use my Star Code Letter Calculator Widget. Below is an example of how to measure a street address. Ignore the part about first and last names for the street value. Prospect Hill comes to the Ten of Spades (Star Code 49).

First Person		
First Name	Middle Name	Last Name
Prospect Hill		
49	0	0 = 49
Suit 1:	**Ten of Spades**	

Second Person		
First Name	Middle Name	Last Name
0	0	0 = 0
Suit 2:	**undefined**	
Composite Suit:	**Ten of Spades**	10♠

| Show Card | Clear |

Star Codes Composites

"Love is space and time measured by the heart." - Marcel Proust

A Composite Star Code is a living, breathing entity created between two or more people, unveiling why they have met. This entity takes on a unique shape and personality with many attributes, forming its harmonic. Star Codes Composites are like portals, entrance and exit points that attract specific emotions and events that vibrationally fit the portal created. Examining family Star Code Composites, friend composites, colleague composites, lover composites, or any group composite is insightful, revealing the significance of the union.

Sometimes, the Star Code Composite can be blamed for the adversities unfolding between people instead of the people who actually create the composite. The same is true for favorable Star Code Composites. This removes some of the shame and blame from relationship struggles. Someone may inadvertently act unkindly in one relationship, for example. Yet, the same person will be as sweet as pie in another relationship. Why do some relationships bring out the best in us while others bring out the worst? Karma gives rise to math, and math doesn't lie. If you are a Truth Seeker, this 52-Star-Code System will inspire you and help you understand yourself, your relationships, and what makes people tick. It's a cosmic language for enlightenment. This is why it's so important who you choose to associate with, partner with, or spend your life with.

Since two or more people create a composite, and we know that composites are portals, how do we activate that portal? It becomes activated by simply thinking of, being with, or communicating with the other. It all begins with a thought or feeling. Portals are magnetic, attracting other identical frequencies, harmonics, and Star Codes. For example, my parents created Star Code Composite 24, the Jack of Clubs, while married. Together, they attracted Jack of Clubs people into their lives, along with events and emotions aligned with the general meanings of that card. They adopted a five-year-old girl born on Jan 29, the day of the Jack of Clubs. She is my sister, Lisa. She brought so much joy into our family. Unfortunately, because my mother was Lisa's Shadow Card, they couldn't see eye to eye and stopped talking when Lisa was 16.

Once, I was at a party with a friend and was asked to run an errand to get more coffee for everyone. One of my friends agreed to accompany me and jumped in the passenger's seat. He was born on Sept 1 as the Ten of Diamonds, Star Code 36. While sitting in the driveway, we created a composite of the Ace of Spades Star Code 40. Here's the math: 36 + 4 = 40. I play the Four of Hearts Star Code 4. Out of nowhere, one of the kids at the party hopped in the backseat of the car to hitch a ride with us. We were both surprised when we turned around to find this coy little girl smiling. She whispered, "I was hoping you wouldn't notice me." She was born on May 5, an Ace of Spades Day Star Code 40. She wanted to escape the party drama and hide with us. She magnetically fit into the portal we created in that car.

Another time, I was at a National Ayurvedic Medical Association annual conference, about to eat lunch in the cafeteria. Scanning around the room with my food tray, I found a large round table with only two people. I sat down, and we had a fabulous, flowing dialogue. No one felt left out. One was born on Nov 6 as Ace of Diamonds Star Code 27. The other was born on May 22 as the Ten of Clubs Star Code 23. Here's the math when we add my Four of Hearts Star Code to the mix: 23 + 4 = 27. Visit the back of this book to find the Star Code Letter Key.

What type of Star Code composite portal do you wish to consciously create in your world with another person? The power is in your hands to shape your relationships. Read more about composites in my relationship book, which will soon be published.

Composite Instructions

When two or more people gather, they form a single separate measurable entity that unveils the nature of the relationship.

Add two or more Star Codes between two people, places, or things, then subtract 52 if the sum is over 52. Use the Star Code Key at the back of the book to find the interfacing card. As a rule of thumb, add your External card to your partner's External card. Then, add your Internal card to your partner's Internal card.

Hypothetical Example: A couple, Maria and Tony, want to know about their Star Code Composite. Add Maria's External Six of Clubs (Star Code 19) to her boyfriend, Tony's External Nine of Clubs (Star Code 22). 19 + 22 = 41, the Two of Spades. The Two of Spades is the Primary Composite Star Code. The same two people will have Internal cards to add to create the Second Composite Star Code. Proceed the same way you did to get the External Star Codes. You will discover your Primary and Secondary Composite Star Codes following these instructions. They both hold weight, but the External one is the most significant.

Finally, when you get the Primary and Secondary Composite Star Codes, you can continue with the addition to determine the

Composite Imprint Code, which was formed from another life-time, realm, or dimension when they were together. This Composite Imprint card will help reveal details of your other lifetime together. Most of us have been incarnating over and over with one another, learning and repeating the same patterns so we can have a second, third, or infinite amount of time to make kinder choices together based on love and not fear.

Please read more about the significance and power of rela-tionships and composite Star Codes in my soon-to-be-published relationship book.

> " I searched for God and found only myself. I searched for myself and found only God. - Rumi

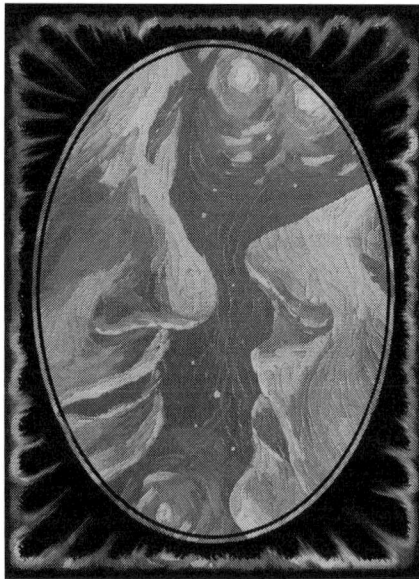

The Black Hole: 9/6 Portal

"Mistakes and adversities are portals of discovery."—Karyn Chabot Martino

Sixes and Nines have reciprocity. They are wobbly. In a state of flux, they can spin upside down to reflect the karmic aspect of a person, thing, place, or event. Just like Masaru Emoto, the Japanese businessperson, author, and pseudoscientist who claimed that human consciousness could affect the molecular structure of water, incoherent emotions can cause the Six and Nine codes to destabilize. For example, a Nine of Spades can be a Six of Spades upside down in someone else's spread, especially when it occupies an unfavorable planetary cycle or if that person is disturbed, ill, or passed on. Even in a favorable planetary cycle, an upside-down Six, posing as a Nine, may represent a completion that is best for all. Example: If a boss plans on firing an essential Six of Hearts employee and comes in for a reading about it, I might predict he will fire his Six of Hearts employee when I see the Nine of Hearts in Saturn in his yearly spread.

Years ago, a friend and card enthusiast, David Suchy, affectionately referred to the 9/6 exchange as a black hole. The 9/6 exchange acted like a black hole and resonated with me, so the name stuck. The science behind black holes is still up for grabs as we continue investigating and understanding these mysterious spiral holes in space. They are designed with the element of surprise, sprinkled with a little karma, and exist at the edge of our time-space continuum. Black holes are timeless, while humans must live within the scope of time. Some of them act like vacuums and never stop spinning. If we apply the principle "As above, so below," we know that the concept of black holes doesn't only apply "up there" but also right here on Earth in our daily lives. They can shape our emotions, spin us, make us invisible at the quantum level, and connect us to other realms, favorable or unfavorable.

They can be seen in nature as sinkholes, rip tides, natural whirlpools in the ocean, maelstroms, and tornadoes. When our star codes transit the 9/6 spot, they can cause our emotional bodies to take on the above-mentioned mysterious afflictions of the Earth. We can track daily, weekly, monthly, yearly, and longer cycles of 9/6 portals using the 45-Quadrations or Robert Lee Camp's card software. Learn more about the Quadrations in my 52 Star Code Student Guide.

Science understands that the Sun curves space, but not enough to create a hole by itself. According to the Schwarzschild solution, the space around the Sun does indeed experience curvature, even if the Sun's mass is spherically symmetric about its center of mass. This is because the mass of the Sun creates a gravitational field, and gravitational fields cause curvature in space. The Earth also curves space, but much less so. Due to the curvatures created by these two celestial bodies, the Sun and the Earth, we can surmise black holes are rooted in the concept of duality. They may be the junction between non-dualistic and dualistic realms. Finally, black holes take shape from the compressed core of a supernova (a giant star exploding at the end of its life). Mass tells space how to curve, and curved space tells mass how to move. I learned this from the EcoTarium Museum of Science and Nature in Worcester, MA.

How can we apply this information practically pertinent to the 52-Star Code measured using the letter value calculator and assigned a Star Code? We can track relocations, property sales, and all sorts of other unfoldings involving property once we have measured its letter value and determined its Code. Suppose you live on Park Ave, which comes to a Nine of Clubs when we add the letter values. You might wonder, "When will I move?" You may move when you see a Six of Clubs occupying a Uranus or Mercury cycle in the yearly spread, especially flanked by 4s and 5s of any suit. Or if the Nine or Six of Clubs occupies the 9/6 spot in your annual card spread. Uranus and Mercury govern property, the 4s and 5s control movement, and the 9/6 Exchange acts like a sinkhole for properties, among other things.

Have you ever seen a car accident or been in one where the person bangs into someone's car, gets out, befuddled, and complains that she didn't notice the other person? The driver might insist that the car just appeared out of nowhere because the vehicle was invisible to her, and consequently, the accident seemed unfair. She may think she was temporarily insane because she might have zero memory of seeing any vehicle at all. On the other hand, the accident victim has no idea what she's talking about. Her only reality is someone side-swiped her. If she had known how to read the 52-Star Codes, she might have noticed that her daily card had passed the 9/6 black hole on the day of the accident. Had she known, she might have driven more carefully, perhaps defensively, knowing that she would have the propensity to go invisible on the road while driving. If someone cared to do the research, I bet a high percentage of all accidents happened on blue or black hole days for the accident victim.

Or suppose you have a Six of Spades lover. When will you break up? Next time you have Nine of Spades in Venus, Mars, or Pluto, look for other cards to provide confluence. Still, the breakup will likely occur when your Six of Spades lover has spun upside down to the Nine of Spades occupying a Venus or Mars cycle in your yearly spread. That person may simply disappear out of the other person's life. I have seen this happen often over the last twenty years of practicing. Another way to predict your Six of Spades lover may leave is if your Star Code Composite occupies the 9/6 spot. The word "spot" refers to the tiny cards found beneath the Direct and Vertical cards in a spread. I go into more detail about this in my 52 Star Code Student Guide.

For example, I had a dear friend for about ten years who betrayed me and broke my heart. We created a Six of Diamonds Star Code Composite. The dissolution of our friendship was tragic for us both, but it was a long time coming in my eyes. I knew our friendship would end when I saw our Six of Diamonds Composite appear as a Nine of Diamonds in my 52-day Venus cycle 2023. My Shadow card, the Four of Spades, occupied a Mercurial 52-day cycle in her yearly spread. That Four of Spades fell into the dreaded 9/6 black hole. She experienced it in

Mercury because it happened so quickly. My Shadow card, the Four of Spades, is the same number as my External card, a Four of Hearts. My Four of Hearts was "Spaded" in her spread and morphed into my Shadow code to solidify the ending. I use "Spaded" as a verb because all the suits have an "action." The Spades end things. It was a fated ending in every sense of a completion.

This ending happened very shortly after I married my Nine of Clubs husband. The Nine of Clubs is the Shadow card to the Six of Diamonds, the composite my friend and I made. Our friendship didn't stand a chance after my marriage. She didn't like my husband, and that was the trigger. We all meet for a season and reason, though it's always hard to say goodbye. I experienced our falling out in a Venus planetary cycle because I loved her so much. Venus is the love planet, platonic or romantic. I still hope for a resolution between us someday. I have silently forgiven her to prevent any more karma and keep my heart free from hatred.

Another constructive way to use the 9/6 portal is for Muhurta, Vedic astrology's divine timing calculator. For example, learning the concept of Muhurta can help us navigate our lives by not planning an essential trip during a 9/6 portal. We can use this Muhurta concept in the 52-Star Code System. Don't make airline reservations on such days or expect to wait in terminals for hours or overnight. Or you may lose your luggage or miss your plane. You may be more vulnerable, and your immune system is weaker on black hole days. As a rule of thumb, black hole cycles cause you to go into quantum invisibility to the rest of the world, where it may feel like you are being ignored, stood up, or simply unimportant. It's best to stay home during such times and meditate. I knew someone who planned their wedding on a 9/6 portal day. Most of their guests didn't show up for unknown reasons. Police swarmed the hotel venue they rented while the owners of the hotel were arrested in the parking lot in front of everyone mysteriously. They had to relocate their reception to another venue at the last minute. Imagine? They could have avoided all this if they understood the concept of Muhurta. Another good reason to learn this is to prevent yourself from having a risky surgery on a black hole day or hire a doctor who might also be in his own daily black hole to perform the surgery. Not good!

You may ask, "When are the Nines simply Nines and Sixes simply Sixes?" When everything in your personal life is kosher, things are in the flow, and you feel authentic and transparent. That's when your External or Internal 6 or 9 of whatever suit you were born with will appear as authentic in someone else's spread. However, they may NOT spin around during a crisis, in some cases. Instead, they may surface in the black hole or be accompanied by one of the black or blue hole cards in the vertical or direction positions when we gaze into the chart of that person experiencing stress. Learn more about vertical and direction positions in my 52 Star Code Student Guide. When we know the External, Internal, Composite, and Imprint codes of the significant people in our lives and understand the nature of the planetary cycles, it's easier to discern a right side up or upside down Six or Nine.

Scientists don't fully understand black holes, stargates, wormholes, or riptides, nor do I. We are not meant to understand them fully because they are wired to be unpredictable. They are designed with the element of surprise, sprinkled with a bit of karma, and exist at the edge of our time-space continuum. They are timeless, while we are mostly trapped inside time unless we teach ourselves to transcend time.

❝ We are multidimensional beings that move effortlessly from one dimension of consciousness to another. We can even be in multiple dimensions at the same time. We don't need an outside portal to get us to the next phase or new earth. You are the portal. Everything is within you. —Karyn Chabot Martino

The Blue Hole: 2/6 Portal

"When the numbers 2 and 6 appear together,
they create the potential for delusion, co-
dependence, drugs, addictions and disorders."
—Karyn Chabot Martino

Much like the 9/6 black hole described above, the 2/6 exchange creates a type of "hole" that is as unpredictable as the 9/6 but has different characteristics and propensities. I nicknamed it the blue hole years ago because I didn't know how to refer to it when explaining it to clients. Names just stick sometimes. It has nothing to do with the color blue either, except I circled it in blue ink once to show my class of students; that's how the nick-name emerged. It's not as threatening as the black hole but just as mysterious. When a card transits through the blue hole, it may indicate altered states, illness, poisons, co-dependence, dysfunction, emotional afflictions, addictions, or drugs. Some-times, people unknowingly put energetic feeding tubes into each other and siphon energy from each other.

What are pips? They are the suit symbols on each card. Notice the pips on the 6 of Spade's card where the two top pips are right side up and the four bottom pips are upside down? The two right-side-up pips symbolically interface with the Two of Spades card. The Six of Spades is the Shadow card to the Two of Spades, much like the Nine of Spades is the Shadow card to the Six of Spades. Notice the four bottom upside pips on the Six of Spade's interfaces with the Four of Spade's card.

Since the Four of Spades card represents health, the only way to identify whether health will be good or bad depends on what planetary cycle it occupies. The Four of Spades indicates health as a theme, unfavorable or favorable. It is up to interpretation, perception, the querent, and the other cards accompanying it for the full story to unfold as favorable or unfavorable. For example, suppose the Four of Spades is the querent's Shadow card. In that case, it tells us the querent will face health challenges most of their life, and the blue and black holes may afflict them more severely than others. When it surfaces, it is more likely to play out as unfavorable, no matter the planetary cycle, only if it's someone's Shadow card for life. It usually gives good results if it's not someone's Shadow card. Still, the details lie in the planetary cycle it is occupying.

If we examine the pips on the Two of Spades, we see the top

pip alone, right side up, as the Ace of Spades. The bottom pip is upside down, symbolically darkening the meaning of the Ace of Spades. The Ace of Spades is the Pluto card for the entire deck, giving flavors of the lower realms, death, metamorphosis, revolution, transformation, secrets, and the occult. The Two of Spades genetically interfaces with the Ace of Spades. Why? The Ace of Spades is the Pluto card for the entire deck and the Moon card for the Two of Spades. It is also a portal representing the mysteries between birth and death, the circle of life, and can often act like a black hole on its own accord.

Since the four pips on the Six of Spades are upside down, our health may go upside down when this card appears. Why? We can see the Four of Spades reflecting on the Six of Spades cards by studying the pips! The Four of Spades also has four pips, two upside down and two right side up, reflecting the Two of Spades blue hole. Since the Six of Spades governs the black and blue holes I am referring to in this chapter, and they both occupy the Neptune row in the Earth Template, we can become blindsided by these portals. Neptune is like smoke and mirrors, hiding in the mist, intentionally creating deception and illusion; nothing solid or predictable can exist when kissed by Neptune. Neptune also governs poisons, toxins, venoms, liquid drugs, oil, confusion, altered states, and grandeur ways of thinking.

We can better understand these portals by examining the subliminal mathematical harmonics under them. The 2/6 portal has Star Codes that add to the Eight of Diamonds Star Code 34. Why is Star Code 34 so significant, as it hides behind the 2/6 portal? Because it represents the entire deck and occupies the highest, most visible, and most powerful place on the Earth Template. This may suggest that when we put power, money, fame, and all that glitters as a priority, it can make us sick by activating the 2/6 blue hole. It's the price we pay for living by delusional priorities. These subliminal harmonics align with our thoughts and code of ethics. If thoughts become things, we must be aware that when we focus on greed, we can fall through the 2/6 blue hole and attract cloudy, blind, unpredictable, sickly, dysfunctional Neptunian experiences.

When we add the Star Codes behind the 9/6 portal, we find the Two of Spades Star Code 41 again. Both portals are intrinsically and intimately connected, but each plays out differently. The black hole tends to make things and people go invisible. The Blue Hole tends to make things wonky and dysfunctional, giving rise to mental, emotional, and physical illness. Interestingly, the Two of Spades ignites the Ace of Spades many times from many angles. What does this tell us? Life is all about relationships and duality. How we interface with one another is probably one of life's most critical and significant mysteries that we should master; hence, the Golden Rule.

The Two of Spades also represents friendship and partnership on the light side, but enemies, power struggles, and co-dependence on the dark side. All these things give rise to how our health will unfold. The significance of how the Ace of Spades (Pluto-death card of the deck) and the Two of Spades (Dualizing the Ace of Spaces) is why Ayurvedic medicine touts, "The root cause of all disease is being in a confused relationship." The key to health is finding clarity concerning who you are (Ace) –relative to the world –and staying in clearly defined relationships (Two) where you know where you stand, what is expected of you, and why you are together and vice versa.

This is particularly helpful when examining the compatibility and harmony of relationships. If you discover your Star Code Composites form a 2 or 6 of any suit, you can know the relationship belongs to the blue hole, filled with lessons, karma, and emotional, mental, and physical illness. Drugs, addiction, co-dependence, and altered states may be involved. The same goes for Star Code Composites, which forms a 6/9. These types of relationships can kill the partners on the dark side or enlighten them if they are already spiritually evolved and working in higher octaves. Learn more about this in my Relationship book and 52 Star Code Student Guidebook.

The Ace-Ten Exchange

Unveil the magic between zero and one and
one and zero.

$$\frac{10}{1}$$

All Aces have a subtle exchange with the Tens of their suit. The number 101 is very significant as it validates the findings within the Ace-Ten Exchange and is the entire premise for how computers work. Computer coding is all based on a specific sequence of Ones and Tens. Quantum physics theories also align with the 1-10 concept. They simultaneously represent the alpha and omega of our number system, the beginning and end. Tens and Aces resonate to the number one, except the Ten has a Zero, which can often spiritualize the Ace by "zeroing-out" the significations of the Ace when it appears in the spread, especially in an unfavorable planetary cycle.

I have had many clients born into the Aces. For example, let's look at an Ace of Clubs client case study. Once, an Ace of Clubs lady asked, "Will my husband divorce me?" I opened her husband's chart and saw that she showed up in his chart as a Ten of Clubs in Venus, Mars, Pluto, or Saturn. If so, that means he plans on "zero-ing" her out of his life, probably by divorce, but we would need other confluence to prove that. If he is cheating on her or abusing drugs, her Ace of Clubs would also show up as a Ten of Clubs in Neptune. Sometimes, a Ten of Hearts in Venus might be interpreted as a wedding, but in some cases, it may indicate the emotional heart is shut down. Hearts can get "zero-ed out." This is especially true if there is also an Ace of Hearts in Pluto or another unfavorable planetary cycle. We need to examine the entire spread before making assumptions or predictions.

All Tens and Aces resonate with the number 1 and interchange. This doesn't mean the Ace person should create and read a birth chart from the Ten of their suit. Instead, this interchange will only appear in the chart of someone who knows the querent. For example, suppose an Exterior Ace of Diamonds woman wants to know how her new online date felt about her on their first meeting. If she appears in his chart at the Ten of Diamonds instead of her authentic Ace of Diamonds occupying an unfavorable planetary cycle? It may indicate he doesn't see her authentically, doesn't like her, or she's putting on a facade. This is especially true if the Ten of Diamonds is accompanied by a Three or Nine, revealing his indecision or his plans never to ask her on another date. It may also indicate he needs to zero her out because he's cheating and wants to keep the date secret.

There are many reasons why the Aces and Tens exchange. Exactly how they appear in their significant other's chart, or someone else's, tells a big part of the story. There would be other supporting cards flanking the Ten or the Ace that would reveal the exchange or disguise, leading to more accuracy and confluence.

The "Ace-Ten" principle can also be applied when encountering the synastry between the signs of Capricorn and Aries. Aries are the 1st sign in the zodiac. Capricorns are the Tenth sign of the zodiac. Therefore, Capricorns are biased toward spiritualizing Aries. When we spiritualize something or someone, we "Zero them out." Zeroing out something or someone may appear as a breakup, division, or disregard for who they indeed are. The Aries might not feel "heard" by the Capricorn, making them feel unseen, unimportant, and small. This may not be intentional, but it is the nature of the dynamic between the Tens and the Ones and Capricorns and Aries. As shown below, the ten has it "over" the one and takes the lead. Read more about this at the beginning of this book under the Ace-Ten Exchange chapter.

> Numbers are the rulers of forms, ideas, and the cause of gods and demons. -Iamblichus

The Two Presence Healers of The Deck

"Love, music and compassionate listening are the greatest healers. That's how presence healing happens."

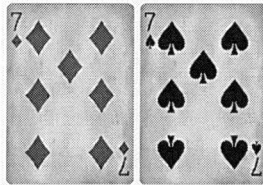

Seven of Diamonds Star Code 33 and Seven of Spades Star Code 46 are Presence Healers.

How and why? The Seven of Diamonds governs 98 particular birthdays out of the 365-day calendar. If you subtract 52 from 98, we get 46, the Seven of Spade's Star Code, revealing the second healer. We always subtract 52 because that is the number of cards in the deck. Ironically, the Seven of Spades is the other "Presence Healer" card that governs another 78 birthdays out of the 365-day calendar. They govern healing portals for 9 Star Codes of 52 potentials, as shown in the bulleted list below. Seven of Spade's folks are the "Primordial Presence Healers" of the deck, indicating they are from the Healer's Soul Family.

People born with the Seven of Diamonds or Seven of Spades cards are naturally "Presence Healers" who simply create the space for people born on the birthdays mentioned above (listed in detail below) to find healing. The people born on the Seven of Diamonds and Seven of Spades birthdays don't have to do anything but be themselves and have an open heart to help others.

> People: She doesn't look sound or act like a healer.
>
> Universe: I'm not looking for actors.

The people associated with the cards in the first list below receive healing when they find themselves in the presence of a Seven of Diamonds person with healing or loving intentions. The people associated with the cards in the second list below receive healing when they find themselves in the presence of a Seven of Spades person with healing or loving intentions. Of course, "intention" is everything, so not much will happen if the Seven of Diamonds person or Seven of Spades person doesn't intend for it or care. Yet, when they do have the intention, the healing will happen for anyone with Internal, External, or Decanate cards listed below. Anyone with a Seven of Diamonds or Seven of Spades External, Internal, Imprint, or Decanate card is also considered a "Presence Healer."

Learn how to calculate your Imprint card at the beginning of the book, or visit my website for the card calculator. If your Imprint card matches any of the cards listed below, you may still receive healing when you meet a Seven of Diamonds or Seven of Spades person, regardless of what layer it fits.

The people associated with the cards listed below receive

healing when they find themselves in the presence of a Seven of Diamonds person with healing or loving intentions. This includes anyone with Internal, External, or Decanate cards listed below. Anyone with a Seven of Diamonds External, Internal, Imprint, or Decanate card is also considered a "Presence Healer."

Seven of Diamond's People are "Presence Healers" for These 98 Birthdays:

- Ace of Clubs Star Code 14 has eight birthdays yearly.
- Five of Spades Star Code 44 has five birthdays yearly.
- Six of Diamonds Star Code 32 has thirteen birthdays yearly.
- Six of Spades Star Code 32 has four birthdays yearly.
- Seven of Clubs Star Code 20 has ten birthdays yearly.
- Seven of Diamonds Star Code 33 has ten birthdays yearly.
- Eight of Clubs Star Code 21 has ten birthdays yearly.
- Eight of Spades Star Code 47 has three birthdays yearly.
- Nine of Diamonds Star Code 35 has nine birthdays yearly.
- Nine of Spades Star Code 48 has four birthdays yearly.
- Jack of Clubs Star Code 24 has twelve birthdays yearly.
- Ten of Diamonds Star Code 36 has nine birthdays yearly.

Seven of Spade's People are "Presence Healers" for these 78 Birthdays:

- Ace of Diamonds Star Code 27 has twelve birthdays yearly.
- Two of Clubs Star Code 15 has eight birthdays yearly.
- Two of Diamonds Star Code 28 has twelve birthdays yearly.
- Two of Spades Star Code 41 has six birthdays yearly.
- Eight of Hearts Star Code 8 has five birthdays yearly.
- Jack of Diamonds Star Code 37 has eight birthdays yearly.
- Queen of Diamonds Star Code 38 has eight birthdays yearly.
- King of Hearts Star Code 13 has seven birthdays yearly.
- King of Clubs Star Code 26 has twelve birthdays yearly.

When we add all the Star Codes in the Seven of Spade's list above, we get 233. Then, we subtract the number 52 repeatedly until we reach the last total hovering just above the number 52. That last hovering number is 77. These double Seven's represent the Seven of Diamonds and the Seven of Spades–the two main Presence Healers of the deck.

❝ *"People start to heal the moment they feel heard."*

I hope the information below sheds light on how and why "Presence Healing" is so powerful. "There are additional ways in which physical presence influences healing. We know, for example, that electromagnetic waves in the form of heat and infrared radiation emanate from the body, especially the hands. Through meditation, biofeedback, and breathing techniques, people can intentionally increase or decrease the amount of this heat and infrared radiation. Infrared radiation, especially at frequencies of 400 to 800 nanometers, is absorbed by a chemical in our cells called cytochrome c. Stimulation of cytochrome c increases the amount of adenosine triphosphate (ATP)—the energy-producing molecule found in all cells.

In dozens of experiments done at Walter Reed Army Institute of Research, investigators found that individuals who put their hands around test tubes containing immune cells while meditating increased the amount of infrared radiation emanating from their hands, stimulating the immune cells to produce more ATP and energy. After this exposure, those cells were more resilient—that is, they survived better when hit with stresses such as heat and chemical shocks.

Remarkably, love-centered meditation and visualization are the most profoundly effective ways to increase our cells' ATP and resilience. Cultivating a feeling of love—such as gratitude, affection, and appreciation—produced the most significant effect. Mental activities such as counting backward or thinking about the weather did not increase ATP or improve cellular resilience."[1]

---

1.   *https://www.psychologytoday.com/us/blog/how-healing-works/202007/how-we-can-help-others-heal-being-present*

Ho'oponopono Forgiveness Novena

Foregiveness does not change the past, but it does enlarge the future. - Paul Boose

This novena can be practiced silently or aloud and is best done alone inside a sacred space. State the <name> of the person you wish to forgive.

Say the following with all your heart:

Please forgive me.
I'm sincerely sorry.
I forgive you.
I love you.
May there be peace between us.
Thank you.

Practice 100 repetitions daily for the first three days, then 50 repetitions per day for the next fourteen days, giving you 1,000 repetitions. This breaks down to ten repetitions each hour for ten hours on the first three days. It will be intense but necessary. For the following 14 days, do ten repetitions five times a day. Use your fingers to count if need be.

If you resist this or feel burnt out halfway through, acknowledge this resistance as the part of you that wants this drama to continue. You will be truly liberated from this entanglement if you genuinely wish to forgive and release the pain, adversities, and other incoherent emotions tangling you to each other.

Practicing the abovementioned steps and following the instructions will help you raise an octave higher, but only if you do it wholeheartedly. It is not WHAT you say, but HOW you say it. Say it like you mean every word, every breath.

If this novena doesn't resonate, try the one below instead. Both are equally powerful, but I can attest first-hand to the one above because it changed my life.

> Our greatest strength lies in the gentleness and tenderness of our hearts. - Rumi

Reasons to Forgive Your Parents

Forgiving does not mean you must invite those who offended you back into your life. Forgiveness happens in your heart and is about you, not the other person. You can love and forgive people from afar, keeping a safe distance with zero animosity while wishing them the best.

- Raising you through their unresolved trauma.
- Not being able to teach you specific skills, because nobody taught them.
- Being emotionally unavailable, as their parents were not emotionally available.
- Doing the best they could with what they knew and had.
- Following cultural norms that they were surrounded with.
- Raising you through their struggles, worries, pain, and fears.
- Trying to be a parent without an instruction manual or directions.
- Never being able to say, "I am sorry."

The Stellar Forgiveness Novena

As we know, forgiveness of oneself is the hardest of all forgivenesses. - Joan Baez

Before you begin this exercise, review and remember the people you have hurt and who have hurt you. I suggest writing this down. Do this exercise sitting or lying down on your back. Create sacred space in whatever way pleases you. Light a soy candle or some clean incense of frankincense, palo santos, or sage to connect you to all the divine elements and ignite your divine guidance.

Step 1. Say aloud: "I would like to exercise forgiveness with myself while I meet my inner child." (Imagine merging with your inner child, embracing them, and becoming one. Envision your inner child standing before you.) I am now undergoing a potent process of aligning my soul with the laws of creation so that we all may be healed. Thank you for being part of my learning to love, respect myself, and release anger and grudges. I, (name), love myself; I have confidence. I learned my lessons and learned to connect with my inner strength. I'm no longer afraid. I'm brave. I am enthusiastic. I am whole. I am happy, abundant, and prosperous. I am satisfied and happy with my achievements. I am accountable for all that has unfolded in my life and realize the light comes through every wound. Everything we have been through together was designed to strengthen me and help me elevate to my most realized self and highest potential of love. I am proud of myself and ask you to connect with me and all these qualities."

Step 2. Say aloud: "I am now going to do a forgiveness exercise. I, <Your Name>, invite <Other Person's Name> to this process of forgiveness: (As you say the name of the person, envision them standing/sitting in front of you)." Then, take a half step towards the person (energetically) and say to them: "Please forgive me for all the hurtful things I did to you in the past, in this incarnation and other incarnations, in all dimensions, in this universe and parallel universes, intentionally and unintentionally. I am sorry. I did not mean to hurt you. Please forgive me. I forgive you, and I love you." Repeat this 5-10 times, if necessary, until you feel inside relaxed and forgiven.

Step 3. Step back (energetically) after you finish the process and tell this person: "Now, I want to tell you about all the hurtful things you did to me." Start by telling them (tell their souls if you choose to do this solo) everything in your heart. Don't leave anything inside. Tell them everything you did not like, things that hurt you, and what you didn't receive or should receive. At this point, it is possible to express yourself as you wish. You can scream, cry, hit a pillow, and so on. Allow the emotions to wash through you like an ocean wave since these emotions do not belong to you.

Step 4. Say aloud: "I forgive you and myself for everything we have done to each other in this incarnation and other incarnations, in this life and other lifetimes, in this dimension and all dimensions, in this universe and parallel universes, intentionally and unintentionally. And now, from this moment on, I release any negative energy connections between us in this incarnation and other incarnations, in this dimension and all dimensions, in this universe and parallel universes, intentionally and unintentionally." Repeating the statement as much as necessary is highly recommended until you feel relieved.

Step 5. Say aloud: I, <name>, am thanking the Loving Creator of All That is, the Innate Intelligence of Nature, the Pure Source of All Creation, and the Infinite Field of All Possibilities where all those who are helpful, loving, and wise exist, for helping me to dissolve, heal, and release me from the following: "I release old beliefs that no longer serve my highest and best. I release all the soul oaths, vows, promises, contracts, alliances, and agreements that connect to those beliefs, intentionally and unintentionally, in this incarnation and other incarnation, in this dimension and all dimensions, in this universe and parallel universes. I am healed and have corrected my actions to find balance, peace, and compassion. I no longer need to jump back on the wheel of karma for another painful incarnation with you.

May you, me, and all beings be happy and free.
Thank you. So Be It.

Prayer of Release

I release my partner from the obligation to complete me. I release my parents from the feeling they failed me. I release my children from the need to bring me pride so they can write their own paths to the rhythm of their hearts. I don't lack anything. I cherish my essence, my way of expressing it, even if not everyone can understand me. I learn from all beings all the time. I honor the divinity in me and you. I heal by releasing, not by suppressing.

Destiny

"Man only suffers because we take seriously what the gods created for fun. We all get stuck into it. We attract what we judge until we no longer judge what we attract. That's the point. Learn to love and accept it. Learn to fall in love with your destiny. Realize that all of it is connected. Every person you meet and every experience you have is divine. If we can notice HOW it is divine. Instead of asking why the Universe did this to me, ask why I chose this for myself. What was the principle I was hoping to learn? And fall in love with that. That's called Amor Fati, the love of destiny. I used to believe in coincidences. I used to believe that my willpower could create whatever I wanted. I used to think there was a juxtaposition between willpower and destiny. But maybe what we call destiny is just the free will of our higher selves." - Robert Edward Grant

52 Star Code Worksheet

Make a list of all your layers of your birthday.
Your main layers are the first five, but each of
them reveals your inner story.

External Card:_____

Internal Cards(s): _____

Shadow Card:_____

Decanate Card:_____

Imprint Card(s):_____

Mirror Card:_____

Primordial Card:_____

Blessed Card:_____

Healing-in Card:_____

Healing-out Card:_____

Higher Octave Card:_____

Exaggerated Card(s):_____

Stress Card(s):_____

Imprint Card(s):_____

First Name Card:_____

Middle Name Card:_____

Last Name Card:_____

Full Birth Name Card:_____

The Earth Template

Mercury							☿

Venus							♀

Mars							♂

Jupiter							♃

Saturn							♄

Uranus							⛢

Neptune							♆

The Spirit Template

Mercury

Venus

Mars

Jupiter

Saturn

Uranus

Neptune

EARTH & SPIRIT
TEMPLATES

	K♣ / K♠	8♦ / Q♠	10♣ / J♠			

A♠ / 7♥	3♦ / 6♥	5♣ / 5♥	10♠ / 4♥	Q♣ / 3♥	A♣ / 2♥	3♥ / A♥	☿
2♥ / A♣	9♠ / K♥	9♣ / Q♥	J♥ / J♥	5♠ / 10♥	7♦ / 9♥	7♥ / 8♥	♀
8♣ / 8♣	J♠ / 7♣	2♦ / 6♣	4♣ / 5♥	6♥ / 4♣	K♦ / 3♣	K♥ / 2♣	♂
A♦ / 2♦	A♥ / A♦	8♠ / K♣	10♦ / Q♣	10♥ / J♣	4♠ / 10♣	6♦ / 9♣	♃
5♦ / 9♦	7♣ / 8♦	9♥ / 7♦	3♣ / 6♦	3♠ / 5♦	5♥ / 4♦	Q♦ / 3♦	♄
J♦ / 3♠	K♣ / 2♠	2♣ / A♠	7♠ / K♦	9♦ / Q♦	J♣ / J♦	Q♠ / 10♦	⊙
Q♥ / 10♠	6♠ / 9♠	6♣ / 8♠	8♥ / 7♠	2♠ / 6♠	4♦ / 5♠	4♥ / 4♠	♆
♆	⊙	♄	♃	♂	♀	☿	

STAR & LETTER CODES

Card	Num	Letter	Card	Num	Letter	Card	Num	Letter	Card	Num	Letter
A ♥	1	a	A ♣	14	n	A ♦	27	A	A ♠	40	N
2 ♥	2	b	2 ♣	15	o	2 ♦	28	B	2 ♠	41	O
3 ♥	3	c	3 ♣	16	p	3 ♦	29	C	3 ♠	42	P
4 ♥	4	d	4 ♣	17	q	4 ♦	30	D	4 ♠	43	Q
5 ♥	5	e	5 ♣	18	r	5 ♦	31	E	5 ♠	44	R
6 ♥	6	f	6 ♣	19	s	6 ♦	32	F	6 ♠	45	S
7 ♥	7	g	7 ♣	20	t	7 ♦	33	G	7 ♠	46	T
8 ♥	8	h	8 ♣	21	u	8 ♦	34	H	8 ♠	47	U
9 ♥	9	i	9 ♣	22	v	9 ♦	35	I	9 ♠	48	V
10 ♥	10	j	10 ♣	23	w	10 ♦	36	J	10 ♠	49	W
J ♥	11	k	J ♣	24	x	J ♦	37	K	J ♠	50	X
Q ♥	12	l	Q ♣	25	y	Q ♦	38	L	Q ♠	51	Y
K ♥	13	m	K ♣	26	z	K ♦	39	M	K ♠	52	Z

52StarCodes.org | 401-680-3934 | Karyn Chabot Martino | Copyright © 2023

Birthday Card Directory

Find your birthday and your associated External and Internal Cards. Next, visit the Star and Letter Codes Chart to discover your corresponding Star Codes. For example, if you were born November 16, Your External Card is 4C—and your Internal Cards are 8C & 8S. Your corresponding Star Codes are 17, 21, and 47. Some birthdays have two Internal Cards, but most have only one.

★

Birthday	Natal External	Internal
January 1	K♠	5♣
January 2	Q♠	K♠
January 3	J♠	10♦
January 4	10♠	7♦
January 5	9♠	4♣
January 6	8♠	3♠
January 7	7♠	4♦
January 8	6♠	3♥
January 9	5♠	K♥
January 10	4♠	A♦
January 11	3♠	J♣
January 12	2♠	10♣
January 13	A♠	9♣
January 14	K♦	8♣
January 15	Q♦	7♣
January 16	J♦	6♣
January 17 Capricorn	10♦	5♥
January 17 Aquarius	10♦	3♠
January 18 Capricorn	9♦	4♥
January 18 Aquarius	9♦	4♦
January 19 Capricorn	8♦	10♠
January 19 Aquarius	8♦	5♣
January 20 Capricorn	7♦	2♥
January 20 Aquarius	7♦	K♥
January 21 Capricorn	6♦	A♥
January 21 Aquarius	6♦	A♦
January 22 Capricorn	5♦	2♣
January 22 Aquarius	5♦	K♣
January 23	4♦	10♣
January 24	3♦	9♣
January 25	2♦	10♦
January 26	A♦	7♣
January 27	K♣	6♣
January 28	Q♣	7♦
January 29	J♣	4♥
January 30	10♣	10♠
January 31	9♣	4♠
February 1	J♠	8♠
February 2	10♠	5♠
February 3	9♠	2♦
February 4	8♠	3♠
February 5	7♠	2♠
February 6	6♠	A♣
February 7	5♠	K♦
February 8	4♠	Q♦
February 9	3♠	9♦
February 10	2♠	8♦
February 11	A♠	9♠
February 12	K♦	6♦
February 13	Q♦	5♦
February 14	J♦	6♠
February 15	10♦	3♠
February 16 Aquarius	9♦	4♦
February 16 Pisces	9♦	2♠
February 17 Aquarius	8♦	5♣
February 17 Pisces	8♦	3♦
February 18 Aquarius	7♦	K♥
February 18 Pisces	7♦	K♦
February 19 Aquarius	6♦	A♦
February 19 Pisces	6♦	Q♦
February 20 Aquarius	5♦	K♣
February 20 Pisces	5♦	J♦

Birthday	Natal External	Internal
February 21 Aquarius	4♦	10♣
February 21 Pisces	4♦	8♦
February 22	3♦	9♠
February 23	2♦	8♠
February 24	A♦	5♦
February 25	K♣	6♠
February 26	Q♣	5♠
February 27	J♣	4♦
February 28	10♣	5♦
February 29 Before noon	10♣	5♦
February 29 After noon	9♠	J♠
March 1	9♠	J♠
March 2	8♠	9♥
March 3	7♠	8♥
March 4	6♠	Q♣
March 5	5♠	6♥
March 6	4♠	5♥
March 7	3♠	7♠
March 8	2♠	K♠
March 9	A♠	2♥
March 10	K♦	4♠
March 11	Q♦	Q♠
March 12	J♦	Q♥
March 13	10♦	3♠
March 14	9♦	2♠
March 15	8♦	3♦
March 16	7♦	K♦
March 17	6♦	Q♦
March 18 Pisces	5♦	J♦
March 18 Aries	5♦	9♦
March 19 Pisces	4♦	8♦

Birthday	Natal External	Internal
March 19 Aries	4♦	6♣
March 20 Pisces	3♦	9♣
March 20 Aries	3♦	7♦
March 21 Pisces	2♦	8♣
March 21 Aries	2♦	6♦
March 22 Pisces	A♦	5♦
March 22 Aries	A♦	3♣
March 23 Pisces	K♣	6♣
March 23 Aries	K♣	4♦
March 24	Q♣	3♦
March 25	J♣	2♣
March 26	10♣	3♥
March 27	9♣	K♥
March 28	8♣	10♥
March 29	7♣	J♣
March 30	6♣	10♣
March 31	5♣	7♥
April 1	7♦	J♦
April 2	6♦	8♦
April 3	5♦	9♠
April 4	4♦	8♠
April 5	3♦	5♦
April 6	2♦	6♣
April 7	A♦	5♦
April 8	K♦	2♦
April 9	Q♦	3♠
April 10	J♦	2♦
April 11	10♦	A♦
April 12	9♦	K♣
April 13	8♦	A♣
April 14	7♦	9♣

Birthday	Natal External	Internal
April 15	6♦	10♦
April 16	5♦	9♦
April 17 Aries	4♦	6♠
April 17 Taurus	4♦	8♥
April 18 Aries	3♦	7♦
April 18 Taurus	3♦	7♥
April 19 Aries	2♦	6♦
April 19 Taurus	2♦	8♠
April 20 Aries	A♦	3♠
April 20 Taurus	A♦	5♥
April 21 Aries	K♣	4♦
April 21 Taurus	K♣	4♥
April 22 Aries	Q♣	3♦
April 22 Taurus	Q♣	5♠
April 23	J♣	7♠
April 24	10♣	K♣
April 25	9♣	2♥
April 26	8♣	4♣
April 27	7♣	Q♣
April 28	6♣	Q♥
April 29	5♣	A♠
April 30	4♣	J♠
May 1	5♣	9♣
May 2	4♣	10♦
May 3	3♣	7♣
May 4	2♣	6♣
May 5	A♣	7♦
May 6	K♦	4♣
May 7	Q♦	3♣
May 8	J♦	4♦
May 9	10♦	A♥

Birthday	Natal External	Internal
May 10	9♦	2♣
May 11	8♦	3♥
May 12	7♦	J♥
May 13	6♦	10♥
May 14	5♦	J♠
May 15	4♦	8♥
May 16	3♦	7♥
May 17	2♦	8♣
May 18 Taurus	A♦	5♥
May 18 Gemini	A♦	Q♦
May 19 Taurus	K♣	4♥
May 19 Gemini	K♣	J♦
May 20 Taurus	Q♣	5♠
May 20 Gemini	Q♣	10♦
May 21 Taurus	J♣	7♠
May 21 Gemini	J♣	9♦
May 22 Taurus	10♣	K♣
May 22 Gemini	10♣	8♣
May 23 Taurus	9♣	2♥
May 23 Gemini	9♣	9♠
May 24	8♣	6♦
May 25	7♣	5♦
May 26	6♣	6♣
May 27	5♣	3♦
May 28	4♣	2♦
May 29	3♣	3♣
May 30	2♣	K♣
May 31	A♣	Q♣
June 1	3♦	9♥
June 2	2♦	8♥
June 3	A♦	7♥

Birthday	Natal External	Internal
June 4	K♦	6♥
June 5	Q♦	5♥
June 6	J♦	4♥
June 7	10♦	8♠
June 8	9♦	7♠
June 9	8♦	K♠
June 10	7♦	5♠
June 11	6♦	4♠
June 12	5♦	Q♠
June 13	4♦	2♠
June 14	3♦	A♠
June 15	2♦	J♠
June 16	A♦	Q♦
June 17	K♣	J♦
June 18 Gemini	Q♣	10♣
June 18 Cancer	Q♣	A♣, 5♠
June 19 Gemini	J♣	9♦
June 19 Cancer	J♣	Q♣, 4♦
June 20 Gemini	10♣	8♦
June 20 Cancer	10♣	Q♥, 5♣
June 21 Gemini	9♣	9♠
June 21 Cancer	9♣	J♥, 2♦
June 22 Gemini	8♣	6♦, J♣
June 22 Cancer	8♣	J♦, A♦
June 23 Gemini	7♣	5♦
June 23 Cancer	7♣	9♥, K♦
June 24	6♣	8♥, A♣
June 25	5♣	10♠, 9♣
June 26	4♣	6♥, 10♦
June 27	3♣	5♥, 9♦
June 28	2♣	7♠, 6♣
June 29	A♣	3♥, 7♦
June 30	K♥	2♥, 6♦
July 1	A♦	3♦, 2♥
July 2	K♦	K♥, 4♣
July 3	Q♦	A♦, Q♣
July 4	J♦	K♣, Q♥
July 5	10♦	10♥, 3♠
July 6	9♦	J♠, 2♠
July 7	8♦	10♠, 3♦
July 8	7♦	7♥, K♦
July 9	6♦	8♠, Q♦
July 10	5♦	7♠, J♦
July 11	4♦	4♥, 8♦
July 12	3♦	5♠, 9♠
July 13	2♦	4♠, 8♠
July 14	A♦	A♥, 5♦
July 15	K♣	2♣, 6♠
July 16	Q♣	A♣, 5♠
July 17	J♣	Q♣, 4♦
July 18	10♣	Q♥, 5♣
July 19	9♣	J♥, 2♦
July 20 Cancer	8♣	J♦, A♦
July 20 Leo	8♣	8♣, A♥
July 21 Cancer	7♣	9♥, K♦
July 21 Leo	7♣	7♠, 2♠
July 22 Cancer	6♣	8♥, A♣
July 22 Leo	6♣	6♠, 3♥
July 23 Cancer	5♣	10♠, 9♣
July 23 Leo	5♣	5♠, J♥
July 24 Cancer	4♣	6♥, 10♦
July 24 Leo	4♣	4♠, 10♥

Birthday	Natal External	Internal
July 25 Cancer	3♥	5♥, 9♦
July 25 Leo	3♣	3♣, J♠
July 26	2♣	2♣, 8♥
July 27	A♠	A♠, 7♥
July 28	K♥	K♥, 8♣
July 29	Q♥	Q♥, Q♣
July 30	J♥	J♥, 6♥
July 31	10♥	10♥, 5♥
August 1	Q♦	Q♦, 5♦
August 2	J♦	J♦, 6♠
August 3	10♦	10♦, 3♠
August 4	9♦	9♦, 4♦
August 5	8♦	8♦, 5♠
August 6	7♦	7♦, K♥
August 7	6♦	6♦, A♦
August 8	5♦	5♦, K♠
August 9	4♦	4♦, 10♣
August 10	3♦	3♦, 9♣
August 11	2♦	2♦, 10♦
August 12	A♦	A♦, 7♣
August 13	K♠	K♠, 6♣
August 14	Q♠	Q♠, 7♦
August 15	J♠	J♠, 4♥
August 16	10♣	10♣, 10♦
August 17	9♣	9♣, 4♠
August 18	8♣	8♣, A♥
August 19	7♣	7♣, 2♣
August 20 Leo	6♣	6♣, 3♥
August 20 Virgo	6♣	6♦
August 21 Leo	5♣	5♣, J♥
August 21 Virgo	5♣	3♦

Birthday	Natal External	Internal
August 22 Leo	4♣	4♣, 10♥
August 22 Virgo	4♣	2♦
August 23 Leo	3♣	3♣, J♠
August 23 Virgo	3♣	3♠
August 24 Leo	2♣	2♣, 8♥
August 24 Virgo	2♣	K♠
August 25 Leo	A♠	A♠, 7♥
August 25 Virgo	A♠	Q♣
August 26	K♥	K♦
August 27	Q♥	10♣
August 28	J♥	9♣
August 29	10♥	10♦
August 30	9♥	7♣
August 31	8♥	6♣
September 1	10♦	8♣
September 2	9♦	7♦
September 3	8♦	K♠
September 4	7♦	5♣
September 5	6♦	4♣
September 6	5♦	Q♣
September 7	4♦	2♣
September 8	3♦	A♠
September 9	2♦	J♠
September 10	A♦	Q♦
September 11	K♣	J♦
September 12	Q♣	10♦
September 13	J♣	9♦
September 14	10♣	8♦
September 15	9♣	9♣
September 16	8♣	6♦
September 17	7♣	5♦

Birthday	Natal External	Internal
September 18	6♣	6♠
September 19	5♣	3♦
September 20 Virgo	4♣	2♦
September 20 Libra	4♣	J♠
September 21 Virgo	3♣	3♠
September 21 Libra	3♣	9♥
September 22 Virgo	2♣	K♠
September 22 Libra	2♣	J♦
September 23 Virgo	A♣	Q♠
September 23 Libra	A♣	10♣
September 24 Virgo	K♥	K♦
September 24 Libra	K♥	6♥
September 25 Virgo	Q♥	10♣
September 25 Libra	Q♥	8♦
September 26	J♥	9♣
September 27	10♥	8♣
September 28	9♥	5♦
September 29	8♥	6♣
September 30	7♥	5♣
October 1	8♦	3♥
October 2	7♦	J♥
October 3	6♦	10♥
October 4	5♦	J♣
October 5	4♦	8♥
October 6	3♦	7♥
October 7	2♦	8♣
October 8	A♦	5♥
October 9	K♣	4♥
October 10	Q♣	5♣
October 11	J♣	7♠
October 12	10♣	K♠

Birthday	Natal External	Internal
October 13	9♣	2♥
October 14	8♣	4♠
October 15	7♣	Q♠
October 16	6♣	Q♥
October 17	5♣	A♠
October 18	4♣	J♠
October 19	3♣	9♥
October 20 Libra	2♣	J♦
October 20 Scorpio	2♣	4♥, 6♠
October 21 Libra	A♣	10♦
October 21 Scorpio	A♣	5♣, 5♠
October 22 Libra	K♥	6♥
October 22 Scorpio	K♥	4♣, 4♠
October 23 Libra	Q♥	8♦
October 23 Scorpio	Q♥	K♠, 5♠
October 24 Libra	J♥	9♠
October 24 Scorpio	J♥	2♥, 2♦
October 25 Libra	10♥	8♠
October 25 Scorpio	10♥	A♥, 3♠
October 26	9♥	Q♠, K♣
October 27	8♥	Q♥, A♠
October 28	7♥	J♥, K♦
October 29	6♥	J♠, 10♦
October 30	5♥	9♥, 9♠
October 31	4♥	8♥, 8♦
November 1	6♦	10♦, 5♥
November 2	5♦	9♦, 4♥
November 3	4♦	6♣, K♠
November 4	3♦	7♦, 2♥
November 5	2♦	6♦, A♥
November 6	A♦	3♣, Q♠

Birthday	Natal External	Internal
November 7	K♣	4♦, Q♥
November 8	Q♣	3♦, J♥
November 9	J♣	2♦, 2♠
November 10	10♣	3♥, 3♦
November 11	9♣	K♥, J♠
November 12	8♣	10♥, Q♦
November 13	7♣	J♣, J♦
November 14	6♣	10♣, Q♣
November 15	5♣	7♥, 9♣
November 16	4♣	8♣, 8♠
November 17	3♣	7♣, 7♠
November 18	2♣	4♥, 6♣
November 19 Scorpio	A♣	5♣, 5♠
November 19 Sagittarius	A♣	3♦
November 20 Scorpio	K♥	4♣, 4♠
November 20 Sagittarius	K♥	2♦
November 21 Scorpio	Q♥	K♣, 5♣
November 21 Sagittarius	Q♥	3♥
November 22 Scorpio	J♥	2♥, 2♦
November 22 Sagittarius	J♥	K♥
November 23 Scorpio	10♥	A♥, 3♠
November 23 Sagittarius	10♥	A♦
November 24 Scorpio	9♥	Q♣, K♣
November 24 Sagittarius	9♥	J♣
November 25	8♥	10♣
November 26	7♥	9♣
November 27	6♥	8♣
November 28	5♥	7♣
November 29	4♥	6♣
November 30	3♥	5♣
December 1	4♦	6♦

Birthday	Natal External	Internal
December 2	3♦	5♣
December 3	2♦	4♣
December 4	A♦	3♣
December 5	K♣	2♣
December 6	Q♣	A♣
December 7	J♣	K♣
December 8	10♣	A♣
December 9	9♣	K♦
December 10	8♣	10♦
December 11	7♣	9♦
December 12	6♣	8♦
December 13	5♣	7♦
December 14	4♣	6♦
December 15	3♣	5♦
December 16	2♣	4♦
December 17	A♣	3♦
December 18	K♥	2♦
December 19 Sagittarius	Q♥	3♥
December 19 Capricorn	Q♥	A♣
December 20 Sagittarius	J♥	K♥
December 20 Capricorn	J♥	K♦
December 21 Sagittarius	10♥	A♦
December 21 Capricorn	10♥	Q♦
December 22 Sagittarius	9♥	J♣
December 22 Capricorn	9♥	9♦
December 23 Sagittarius	8♥	10♣
December 23 Capricorn	8♥	8♦
December 24 Sagittarius	7♥	9♣
December 24 Capricorn	7♥	9♠
December 25	6♥	6♦
December 26	5♥	5♦
December 27	4♥	6♣
December 28	3♥	3♦
December 29	2♥	2♦
December 30	A♥	3♦
December 31 Before noon	A♥	3♠
December 31 After noon	K♠	5♣

About the Author

It's always a challenge to toot your own horn and organize your entire past into small, coherent paragraphs. So, I asked a friend (Thank you, Ceciley!) to write this humble biography for me instead: In the 1990s, Karyn became a mother, professional dance instructor, performer, and nationally certified yoga teacher. 1995, she graduated from Goddard College with a bachelor's degree in health and nutrition. In 1997, she graduated from The Ayurvedic Institute in New Mexico while simultaneously graduating from Universal Massage Therapeutics of New Mexico. In 1998, after healing from several genetic auto-immune diseases, she was the first to offer professional massage therapy and Ayurvedic health counseling in Newport, RI. In 1999, she invented Sacred Stone Massage Therapy while renting a house on a gorgeous stone beach in RI. She certified over 3,000 Sacred Stone Therapists over the next ten years, awarding continuing education credits from the NCBTMB and NAMA. The RIOPC approved her Sacred Stone School and Center in 2012. In 2003, she became a National Ayurvedic Medical Association member and achieved the Practitioner level. Fox TV interviewed her and aired Sacred

Stone Therapy on their Living Better channel in 2004. She published many articles in peer-reviewed trade journals while Sacred Stone Therapy was featured on the cover of the American Massage Therapy Association Magazine in October 2003 and March 2005.

While she trained the staff at many international and national spas and schools during her forties, she also presented at leading industry conferences like the National Ayurvedic Medical Association and the American Massage Therapy Association. She produced eight comprehensive professional instructional DVDs on the art of stone medicine, massage, and Ayurvedic spa therapies. She wrote over twenty illustrated instructional books and nineteen online continuing education courses approved by the NCBTMB for massage therapists and Ayurvedic Practitioners. By 1999, she trained as one of the first Ayur*Yoga Instructors from the Ayurvedic Institute and Ayurveda-Yoga Institute of NYC. She founded one of the first approved Yoga Alliance Schools in RI in 2013 while earning certifications in Reiki, Quantum Touch, Fitness Training, Nutrition, Shamanism, Spirit Rescue Mediumship, Bodytalk Systems Level 3, Marma Point Therapy, Pancha Karma Therapies, Cranio-Sacral Therapy, Chinese Cupping, Yuen Method, Medical Thai Therapy; Ayurvedic Aesthetics and Colon Hydrotherapy.

In 2002, she embarked on an 8-year astrology study quest, earning her certification in Ancient Ayurvedic Astrology with Gandharva Sauls. She became an adjunct faculty professor at Bristol Community College in 2003 and began studying the 52 Star Code System under Robert Lee Camp. In 2007, she studied at the master's level at Maharishi University in Vedic Science and was initiated as a Sidha in the Transcendental Meditation lineage. In 2008, she met Thomas Morrell in Iowa, author of The Ancient Book of Time, deepening her card studies. She continued studying Vedic astrology with David

Hawthorne in Iowa and at the Arsha Vidya Ashram in PA. In 2011, she earned a master's in writing and Ayurvedic medicine from Goddard College, inspiring her to open an Ayurvedic Health Counselor Program as part of Sacred Stone School. 2012, she founded RI's first private, state-approved, proprietary Ayurvedic massage therapy school. By 2018, after immersing herself in the science of the stars for so long, Karyn's intuition heightened, and she began channeling primordial Star Code formulas. As a result, Karyn started teaching Vedic astrology and the 52 Star Code System and continues to write books, counsel, and teach to share her knowledge. She is a monthly astrology blogger for three local magazines and plans to launch the *Star Code School* online by the end of 2024.

Visit 52StarCodes.org

f facebook.com/karyn.chabot.martino
X x.com/SAMA_RI
instagram.com/52starcodes

Index

Gratitude — vii

AUTHOR'S NOTE — 1
Thank you for reading my book. I hope it provides profound insights into who you are and the relationships that have made you who you are today.

Preface — 3

Introduction — 9

HOW TO USE THIS BOOK — 17
In the sunlight of awareness, all things become sacred. - Thich Nhat Hahn

ARE YOU A CUSPER? — 23
"At the midnight hour, I can feel your power." -Madonna

GENESIS OF THE SUITS: THE ANKH — 26
The ancient key representing birth, death and the mysteries inbetween.

Hearts — 29

Clubs — 30

Diamonds — 31

Spades — 32

EVOLUTION OF THE SUITS — 35
The Tao gives birth to One. One gives birth to Two. Two gives birth to Three. Three gives birth to all things. — Tao Te Ching

STAR CODE TERMINOLOGY — 37
What we know is a drop. What we don't know is an ocean. - Isaac Newton

External Cards — 37

Internal Cards — 41

Decanate Ruling Cards — 42

Mirror Cards — 42

Shadow Cards — 44

Primordial Cards — 47

Stress Cards — 49

Blessed Cards — 52

The Blessed Trumped the Stressed! — 55

Blessed Cards in Unfavorable Planetary Cycles — 56

When Blessed Meets Stressed 57

Exaggerated Cards 58

The Royal Family 61

Imprint Cards 63

Higher Octave Cards 70

Healing-in Cards 75

Healing-out Cards 77

ALL THE LAYERS 78
The infinite vibratory levels, the dimensions of interconnectedness are without end. There is nothing independent. All beings and things are residents in your awareness. - Alex Grey

WHEN A CARD APPEARS 84
Nothing happens by chance.

SOUL GENEALOGY 90
When the Grandmothers speak, the earth will be healed. - Hopi Proverb

Record Your Family Layers 92

THE REIGN OF THE 8 OF DIAMONDS 98

What is an Analemma? 98

GOLDEN RULE 102
Surround yourself with people who make you happy. People who make you laugh, who help you when you're in need. People who genuinely care. They are the ones worth keeping in your life. Everyone else is just passing through.–Karl Marx

STARGATE EXPLORATION 104
There is a way from me to you that I am constantly searching for. - Rumi

STARGATE BIRTHDAYS 108
Are you a "Walking Stargate?" Do you belong to the Stargate Family?

STARGATE CASE STUDY 116
She ignited the only Stargate that rules the Mother Wound when she chose May 26th as her wedding day.

THE MOTHER WOUND 125
The more a daughter knows the details of her mother's life, the stronger the daughter. - Anita Diamant

Mother-Goddess-Wound Cards 128

GENDERS AND THE SUITS 134
"What is straight? A line can be straight, or a street, but the human heart, oh, no, it's curved like a road through mountains." Tennessee Williams

The Reversed Gender Card People 134

THE TRINE OF DECEPTION   138
"One who decieves will always find those who allow themselves to be decieved." -Niccolo Machiavelli

FAVORABLE AND UNFAVORABLE PLANETARY CYCLES   140
"Beyond all ideas of good and bad, right or wrong, there is a field. I'll meet you there." - Rumi

HALLOWED BE THY NAME: LETTER VALUES   145
Hate has four letters, but so does Love. Enemies have seven letters, but so does Friends. Lying has five letters, but so does Truth. Cry has three letters, but so does Joy. Negativity has ten letters, but so does Positivity.

STAR CODES COMPOSITES   150
"Love is space and time measured by the heart." - Marcel Proust

COMPOSITE INSTRUCTIONS   153
When two or more people gather, they form a single separate measurable entity that unveils the nature of the relationship.

THE BLACK HOLE: 9/6 PORTAL   155
"Mistakes and adversities are portals of discovery."—Karyn Chabot Martino

THE BLUE HOLE: 2/6 PORTAL   162
"When the numbers 2 and 6 appear together, they create the potential for delusion, co-dependence, drugs, addictions and disorders." —Karyn Chabot Martino

THE ACE-TEN EXCHANGE   167
Unveil the magic between zero and one and one and zero.

THE TWO PRESENCE HEALERS OF THE DECK   170
"Love, music and compassionate listening are the greatest healers. That's how presence healing happens."

Seven of Diamond's People are "Presence Healers" for These 98 Birthdays: 172

Seven of Spade's People are "Presence Healers" for these 78 Birthdays: 173

HO'OPONOPONO FORGIVENESS NOVENA   175
Foregiveness does not change the past, but it does enlarge the future. - Paul Boose

REASONS TO FORGIVE YOUR PARENTS   177
Forgiving does not mean you must invite those who offended you back into your life. Forgiveness happens in your heart and is about you, not the other person. You can love and forgive people from afar, keeping a safe distance with zero animosity while wishing them the best.

THE STELLAR FORGIVENESS NOVENA   178
As we know, forgiveness of oneself is the hardest of all
forgivenesses. - Joan Baez

Prayer of Release   181

Destiny   181

52 Star Code Worksheet   183

BIRTHDAY CARD DIRECTORY   192
Find your birthday and your associated External and Internal
Cards. Next, visit the Star and Letter Codes Chart to
discover your corresponding Star Codes. For example, if you
were born November 16, Your External Card is 4C—and your
Internal Cards are 8C & 8S. Your corresponding Star Codes
are 17, 21, and 47. Some birthdays have two Internal Cards,
but most have only one.

About the Author   207

28972080R10124